English in Europe Today

AILA Applied Linguistics Series (AALS)

The AILA Applied Linguistics Series (AALS) provides a forum for established scholars in any area of Applied Linguistics. The series aims at representing the field in its diversity. It covers different topics in applied linguistics from a multidisciplinary approach and it aims at including different theoretical and methodological perspectives. As an official publication of AILA the series will include contributors from different geographical and linguistic backgrounds. The volumes in the series should be of high quality; they should break new ground and stimulate further research in Applied Linguistics.

Editor

Susanne Niemeier
University of Koblenz-Landau

Editorial Board

Jean-Marc Dewaele
University of London

Nancy H. Hornberger
University of Pennsylvania

Folkert Kuiken
University of Amsterdam

Rosa M. Manchón
University of Murcia

Françoise Salager-Meyer
Universidad de los Andes, Merída

Volume 8

English in Europe Today. Sociocultural and educational perspectives
Edited by Annick De Houwer and Antje Wilton

English in Europe Today

Sociocultural and educational perspectives

Edited by

Annick De Houwer
University of Erfurt

Antje Wilton
University of Siegen

John Benjamins Publishing Company
Amsterdam / Philadelphia

™ The paper used in this publication meets the minimum requirements of American National Standard for Information Sciences – Permanence of Paper for Printed Library Materials, ANSI z39.48-1984.

Library of Congress Cataloging-in-Publication Data

English in Europe today : sociocultural and educational perspectives / edited by Annick De Houwer, Antje Wilton.
    p.   cm. (AILA Applied Linguistics Series, ISSN 1875-1113 ; v. 8)
Includes bibliographical references and index.
1. English language--Study and teaching--Europe. 2. English language--Europe. 3. English language--Influence on foreign languages. 4. Languages in contact. I. De Houwer, Annick. II. Wilton, Antje.
PE2751.E5554   2011
428.0071'04--dc22   2010043365
ISBN 978 90 272 0524 7   (Hb ; alk. paper)
ISBN 978 90 272 8734 2   (Eb)

John Benjamins Publishing Co. · P.O. Box 36224 · 1020 ME Amsterdam · The Netherlands
John Benjamins North America · P.O. Box 27519 · Philadelphia PA 19118-0519 · USA

Dedication

We dedicate this volume to Karlfried Knapp, our valued colleague and friend, on the occasion of his official retirement from the University of Erfurt in 2011. Karlfried Knapp has devoted a considerable amount of his research and teaching activity to the English language, be it in its role as a *lingua franca* or as a language to be acquired through formal schooling. Karlfried Knapp's vested interest in applied linguistics internationally and in Europe in particular is well illustrated by his initiation of AILA-Europe, the European regional network within the International Association of Applied Linguistics. Karlfried was Secretary General of AILA from 2002 until 2008. One of his most recent major achievements is the co-editing of Mouton de Gruyter's series of Handbooks of Applied Linguistics.

Karlfried's long-standing connection with AILA makes it particularly appropriate that this volume is being published in the official AILA book series, the AILA Applied Linguistics Series.

The contributors to this volume all have either a personal and/or a professional connection with Karlfried and contributed their chapters in honor of his service to the field.

Annick De Houwer and Antje Wilton, Erfurt, July 2010

Table of contents

List of contributors

Jasone Cenoz
Department of Research Methods
in Education
University of the Basque Country
Tolosa Hiribidea 70
20018 Donostia-San Sebastian
Spain
jasone.cenoz@ehu.es

Kees de Bot
Departments of English and
Applied Linguistics
University of Groningen
Oude Kijk in 't Jatstraat 26
9712 EK Groningen
The Netherlands
C.L.J.de.Bot@rug.nl

Annick De Houwer
Department of Linguistics
University of Erfurt
Nordhäuser Str. 63
D-99089 Erfurt
Germany
annick.dehouwer@uni-erfurt.de

Susan M. Gass
English Language Center
Michigan State University
A 714 Wells Hall
E. Lansing, MI 48824-1027
USA
gass@msu.edu

Annelie Knapp
English Department
University of Siegen
Adolf-Reichwein-Str. 2
57076 Siegen
Germany
knapp@anglistik.uni-siegen.de

Kurt Kohn
English Department
University of Tübingen
Wilhelmstr. 50
72074 Tübingen
Germany
kurt.kohn@uni-tuebingen.de

Li Wei
Department of Applied Linguistics and
Communication
Birkbeck College
University of London
43 Gordon Square
London WC1H 0PD
United Kingdom
li.wei@bbk.ac.uk

Jacomine Nortier
Department of Linguistics
University of Utrecht
Trans 10
3512 JK Utrecht
The Netherlands
j.m.nortier@uu.nl

Daniel Reed
English Language Center
Michigan State University
A 714 Wells Hall
E. Lansing, MI 48824-1027
USA
reeddan@msu.edu

Barbara Seidlhofer
Department of English
University of Vienna
Spitalgasse 2–4 / Hof 8.3
1090 Wien
Austria
barbara.seidlhofer@univie.ac.at

Eva van Rein
Departments of English and
Applied Linguistics
University of Groningen
Oude Kijk in 't Jatstraat 26
9712 EK Groningen
The Netherlands
E.M.J.van.Rein@student.rug.nl

Marjolijn H. Verspoor
Departments of English and
Applied Linguistics
University of Groningen
Oude Kijk in 't Jatstraat 26
9712 EK Groningen
The Netherlands
M.H.Verspoor@rug.nl

Antje Wilton
English Department
University of Siegen
Adolf-Reichwein-Str. 2
57076 Siegen
Germany
wilton@anglistik.uni-siegen.de

Acknowledgement

We are grateful to Kees Vaes from John Benjamins and Susanne Niemeier, our book series editor, and the AALS editorial board for giving us the opportunity to honor Karlfried Knapp in this highly visible international forum.

We would also like to thank our contributors for their enthusiastic and supportive cooperation.

The dynamics of English in a multilingual Europe

Antje Wilton and Annick De Houwer
University of Siegen / University of Erfurt, Germany

Throughout European history, multilingualism has coexisted with one or more *linguae francae*. Today's European *lingua franca* is English, and it, too, functions within a thoroughly multilingual context. This introduction to the volume *English in Europe Today* illuminates some of the sociocultural and educational contexts in which English and its manifestations in the European linguistic landscape play a shaping role. The contributions to the volume are set within these varied contexts. Together they bear witness to the challenging but enriching dynamics that are part and parcel of the use of English in multilingual Europe today.

Europe has been multilingual for at least 2.5 millennia (Green 1998). With changing patterns of migration, warfare and the wielding of power, language contact situations within Europe have been constantly changing, too. Conversely, patterns of linguistic change reflect different power structures and societal realities.

Typically, language contact situations leave their traces in the respective languages' lexicons. The direction of the import of loanwords signals which of the languages involved is the more influential (e.g., Field 2002: 4). When language A imports relatively more words from language B than the other way round, language B is the more influential one. This imbalance reflects the fact that the group of people associated with the more influential language is usually seen as more powerful or economically and culturally superior (e.g., Thomason 2001). When power relations change, patterns of lexical borrowing do, too.

Some of the earliest records of language use in Europe show evidence of this dynamic. For instance, from about 500 BC to the first century AD, Germanic imported many loanwords from Celtic, but hardly the other way round. This was a time when Celtic civilization was politically and culturally much stronger than anything the Germanic tribes could offer (Green 1998: 145ff.). Similarly, the import of Latin word stock into Germanic was far greater during the period of Roman rule in Europe than the other way around:

> Although this linguistic traffic ran in two ways the dominance of the Romans for some centuries and the superiority of their civilization meant that the influence of Latin on Germanic was decisive and considerable, whilst that of Germanic on Latin was slight.　　　　　　　　　　　　　　　　　　　　(Green 1998:183)

In contrast, by ca. 400 AD, when the Roman Empire was starting to decline as a partial result of the increased political power of the Germanic Franks, more and more Germanic words were imported into Latin (Green 1998:193ff.).

Latin did, of course, continue to exert quite some influence on the other languages in Europe throughout the Middle Ages. In the Renaissance period the renewed interest in classical ideas expressed in Latin and Greek texts coincided with their incorporation into the different languages of Europe, including English (e.g., Baugh & Cable 1978). This raised issues relating to the import of lexical items from Latin (or Greek) into other languages. In Renaissance England, for instance, there was a vehement scholarly controversy between propagators and opponents of the deliberate incorporation of Latin or Latin-based terms into the English language. The controversy centered around the question whether words were being 'taken over by one language from another in answer to a definite need' (Baugh & Cable 1978:84) or whether they were a danger to the purity and expressiveness of the receiving language, as expressed in this quote from 1561:

> I am of this opinion that our own tung shold be written cleane and pure, unmixt and unmangeled with borowing of other tunges, wherin if we take not heed by tijm, ever borowing and never payeng, she shall be fain to keep her house as bankrupt.　　　　　　　　　　　　(Sir John Cheke in Hoby 1561/1967:12)

In present-day Europe, similar controversies exist, but now with regard to imports from English into other European languages, also known as Anglicisms. This topic is, for instance, hotly debated in Germany, where it regularly features in the media (see for instance the news items on the website of the *Verein Deutsche Sprache* (German Language Association) at http://www.vds-ev.de/).

The issue of linguistic borrowing as a threat is taken up in the contribution by Jacomine Nortier (this volume), who illuminates the conflicting effects that English as language with high prestige has on public perception in the Netherlands. Amongst others, Nortier shows that there is a fear of Dutch losing out to English, and although this might be the case in some areas of life where English is steadily gaining ground, the author concludes that Dutch is by no means in danger. It is interesting to note, though, that a fear of loss of the native or national language is present in a country whose inhabitants are generally renowned for their excellent command of English and in which, compared to other areas in Europe, English is present in many aspects of everyday life. To uninformed outsiders, this pervasive proficiency and use signal either a sure confidence about the security of the native language, or a lack of concern for it.

The fear that Dutch might be threatened by English is also shared by many Dutch speakers living in Flanders who are also generally quite proficient in English. This fear does not take into account that never before, Dutch has been used in so many different circumstances as today or has been learned as a second language by so many people as today. This is true of many other European languages as well. The main reasons lie in the far greater access to higher education in Europe since the end of World War II, the highly increased rates of immigration from outside Europe since the 1960's, and, more recently, the advent of new technologies such as the internet and mobile telephones which have greatly increased the amount of language that is used overall.

Nortier (this volume) calls Dutch a 'small' language in the context of the European Union. While there certainly are 'bigger' European languages in terms of the number of first and second language speakers, there are many languages with a much smaller population base than Dutch. If we look only at those European languages that are official languages in the context of the European Union, Dutch is bigger than 16 other current official EU languages (Table 1). Official EU languages are languages 'to be used by the European Economic Community' (see Regulation No 1 determining the languages to be used by the European Economic Community, cf. http://eur-lex.europa.eu/LexUriServ/LexUriServ.do?uri= CONSLEG:1958R0001:20070101:EN:PDF).

Of course, Dutch is fairly 'small' compared to, for instance, French, Spanish and German in terms of the geographical area where it is used and in terms of its use by speakers living outside that geographical area. As Nortier's contribution shows, this 'smallness' is reflected at official EU meetings in Brussels. Quite clearly, English is the language that is often used there instead of Dutch.

Having to deal with 23 languages at the level of EU institutions represents a formidable language management problem (cf. also Nortier, this volume). The actual reality of European multilingualism is still much more complex. Within the borders of the European Union there are many more languages that are being used than just the 23 official EU languages. There are many additional, traditionally European languages such as Basque (cf. the contribution by Jasone Cenoz, this volume), Welsh and Sorbian. For detailed overviews of many of these languages in European countries both within and outside of current EU borders, see Goebl, Nelde, Stary & Wölck (1996); the more recent volume by Ó Riagáin (2006) addresses some of the educational issues involved.

Table 1. The estimated number of speakers of each of the 23 official EU languages (February 2010)

Official EU language	EU country/countries where the official EU language is a national or official language	Estimated number of speakers in millions*
Maltese	Malta	0.3
Irish	Ireland	0.5
Estonian	Estonia	1.3
Slovenian	Slovenia	2.0
Latvian	Latvia	2.3
Lithuanian	Lithuania	3.3
Finnish	Finland	5.0
Slovak	Slovakia	5.4
Danish	Denmark	5.5
Bulgarian	Bulgaria	7.6
Swedish	Sweden, Finland	9.5
Hungarian	Hungary	10.0
Czech	Czech Republic	10.5
Portuguese	Portugal	10.6
Greek	Greece, Cyprus	12.0
Romanian	Romania	21.5
Dutch	the Netherlands, Belgium	22.9
Polish	Poland	38.1
Spanish	Spain	45.8
Italian	Italy	60.0
English	United Kingdom, Ireland, Malta	65.8
French	France, Luxemburg, Belgium	68.7
German	Germany, Austria, Luxemburg, Belgium	90.6

* Here assumed to coincide with the entire population of a country as listed on the official EU website http://europa.eu/abc/european_countries/eu_members/ in February 2010 or, in the case of more than one official EU language per country, based on rough estimates of the portions of the population purportedly mainly speaking one or the other language; problematic for estimates here is the fact that many people use two languages on a daily basis and, conversely, that people may claim to know a language but hardly ever actually use it; these estimates also ignore the fact that many inhabitants of the EU do not necessarily use any of the official EU languages on a daily basis.

EU-internal migration such as that of Italian workers to Denmark, Polish workers to the United Kingdom or German and British pensioners to Spain have greatly added to the linguistic diversity one can find in any region in the EU. Then there is of course the immigration into the EU from both other European and non-European people, such as that by Bosnians to Belgium or Algerians to France. All these migration patterns give rise to changed linguistic situations (e.g., Extra & Verhoeven 1993; Wilton 2009). For studies documenting some of the linguistic diversity in the EU today, see De Houwer (2003), Deprez (1995) and Extra & Yagmur (2004). European countries that do not belong to the EU such as Norway, Switzerland and Turkey have also seen an increase and diversification of the languages spoken in their territories (cf. respectively, Lanza & Svendsen 2007; Dürmüller 1997 and Karahan 2005). Never before has Europe been as multilingual as it is today (cf. also Extra & Gorter 2008).

In European language history, the changing patterns of linguistic diversity and political power have given rise to a number of languages gaining a wider than regional currency. The establishment of Latin as a *lingua franca* in most parts of the Roman Empire was promoted by a number of factors such as the dominance of Roman political, economical, technological and military power, cultural superiority and the development of a literary tradition. Latin shared the role of a European *lingua franca* with Greek, which was the main language of wider communication in the Eastern provinces of the Roman Empire.

Latin continued to be used as a *lingua franca* throughout the Middle Ages and the Renaissance period. As such, it served different speech communities and various domains of discourse (Haye 2005; Maass & Volmer 2005). With the rise of the so-called vernacular languages as literary languages in Europe (Fishman 2010) and the establishment of national languages in early modern European history (Gardt 2000) other languages than Latin were increasingly used as *linguae francae* in certain areas of public and private life. Obvious examples are the use of French as the language of diplomacy and German as a supra-regional *lingua franca* as well as an international language of learning and modern science (Carli & Ammon 2008). Especially with the advent of the Soviet state, Russian became a major *lingua franca* in Eastern Europe (Pavlenko 2006).

So far, none of the *linguae francae* that were dominant in large areas of Europe at any one time, be they Latin, Greek, French, German or Russian, have managed to threaten European multilingualism in any serious way. In fact, the use of Latin was at the root of the development of multiple languages that we now know as Italian, Spanish, Catalan, French, Rumanian and Portuguese (Adams 2007; Wright 2004). Although the Roman Empire and the concomitant use of Latin reached far into the areas of Europe where Greek was being used as a *lingua franca* alongside Latin, Greek itself was firmly established both in Roman education and in the administration of the Eastern provinces (Adams 2003b: 186). What is more, Latin-Greek bilingualism was at the core of what constituted intellectual life far into the Middle Ages (Adams 2003a; Maass & Volmer 2005). Educated people throughout Europe were at least bilingual in Latin or Greek plus an additional language (Karahan 2005; Kremnitz 1990).

Similarly, English is currently a *lingua franca* that educated people throughout Europe are expected to know, in addition to any other European language (e.g., House 2008). Others would agree that "the use of an international language of communication, as for example English as a lingua franca, is [..] a precondition for pan-European communication and cooperation" (Karlfried Knapp, quoted in Cali; Stegu & Vetter 2008: 132). For many, however, the continuing spread of English geographically, functionally, and in terms of its permeation of society is seen as a hindrance to active multilingualism and as a threat to linguistic diversity (Ehlich 2009). This point is taken up in the contribution by Barbara Seidlhofer (this volume). Seidlhofer argues for a reconceptualization of English in order to solve the dilemma of linguistic diversity on the one hand, and the creation of a sense of communal integration on the other. English needs to be seen as an enrichment of the linguistic repertoire of Europe, not a threat to its diversity.

Ambivalent attitudes to high prestige languages have been common throughout European history. Roman attitudes to Greek, for instance, were also ambivalent: on the one hand, Greek was the only language that the Romans of Antiquity considered worth learning (Quintilian, I, 1, XII–XIV), but on the other hand, there were times when Romans regarded a too extensive use of Greek, in particular on public occasions, with suspicion (Adams 2003a: 11). As shown in the contribution by Kurt Kohn (this volume), similarly ambivalent attitudes towards English in Europe today are reflected in the tension between upholding 'standard English' as a goal for English language teaching and the reality of so-called non-native speaker use of English as a *lingua franca*. Kohn explores the question of who it is that really 'owns' English, and proposes a social constructionist approach to the use of English in *lingua franca* situations that offers a welcome counterweight to the increasingly outdated idea of linguistic imperialism (as also discussed in House 2008).

The social constructionist approach to the type of English that is or should be targeted in English language learning in Europe as proposed in this volume by Kohn (and, to a lesser degree, by Seidlhofer) stands in contrast to the unquestioned adoption of the American or British English native speaker standard in many curricula in Europe (see, e.g., the teaching curriculum for English as a first language in some German grammar schools, Ministerium für Kultus, Jugend und Sport Baden-Württemberg 2004: 111). The co-existence of quite opposing views of what variety of English is appropriate as a target for language use shows the continuing ambivalence towards English in Europe.

Whatever variety of English is used – one has to learn it. In Great Britain and Ireland, many people learn a variety of English as a first language at home when they are children (L1; however, as Graddol (2006) noted, this number has been declining; following Caruana (2007) there are most likely a fair number of children who acquire English as an L1 in Malta as well). In the rest of Europe, children of expatriate English-speaking parents will generally also grow up with English as an L1 in the home.

In order to cater for the education of children of expatriate English-speaking parents, there are many private, English-speaking schools throughout Europe, from Belgium to Turkey, and from Norway to Spain. Children of non-English-speaking parents are generally welcome in these schools, too (as long as the high tuition fees are paid!). Susan Gass and Daniel Reed (this volume) discuss English test development in one such school in Greece. We come back to their contribution later in this chapter.

Let us take a look at international private schools in the Brussels area in Belgium. Brussels has many international institutions and companies. The international expatriate community is accordingly large (as is also the case in other major European cities such as Frankfurt and Paris). The Brussels area boasts five major international, English-medium schools and a string of smaller private schools that offer instruction through English or through English and French (e.g., see listings on http://www.expatica.com and in *The Bulletin*, an English-medium Belgian weekly magazine aimed primarily at an upwardly mobile international readership). In contrast, there is only a single international school in Brussels that offers full German-medium instruction, and none that offer full Italian- or Spanish-medium instruction, for instance.

However, German, Italian and Spanish, in addition to all the other official EU languages, are on offer as a medium of instruction within the international European School system (see, e.g., http://www.eeb1.org). The European Schools, which are primarily aimed at children of employees who work for the European Union institutions, are very multilingual, and their stated aim is to contribute towards children's development as multilingual individuals (Baetens Beardsmore 1993). Interestingly, the European Schools' logo is in Latin (*Schola Europaea*). English has no special status in the European School curriculum: as their first foreign language, pupils have the free choice amongst English, French, German or Spanish (Latin is also on offer, but is part of a package of choice with either Music or Art). At present, there are 14 European Schools in seven European countries that cater for about 21,000 pupils per year (see the official website of the European Schools, http://www.eursc.eu/).

The majority of children in Europe do not attend international schools, though. Rather, they attend local schools that usually have as their medium of instruction the language of the region they are located in, or, in some officially bilingual communities, two languages. European countries differ from each other in the precise policies they adopt for the teaching of second, third or fourth languages. The choice of languages on offer varies, as do the ages or school grades at which they are offered. We return to a discussion of these below, after picking up again on where we left off earlier, namely on our brief outline of settings in which children may learn English as an L1.

Both in Great Britain and Ireland and in continental Europe, children in bilingual families may grow up with English as an L1 in the home in addition to another language that is being learned as an L1 (Bilingual First Language Acquisition or BFLA, see De Houwer 2009a, 2009b). There is both anecdotal and research evidence suggesting that the number of families who use English at home but who have no family ties with an English-speaking country is on the rise. More and more young parents in continental Europe with the same monolingual language background who have learned English as an L2 apparently decide to speak English to their offspring, in addition to or instead of their L1 (second author's informal observations). Research evidence from a large survey of language use in approximately 18,000 families in the officially Dutch-speaking region of Flanders, Belgium (De Houwer 2003) supports this: English featured among the top 4 languages being spoken in the bilingual and multilingual families that were part of the sample (besides French, Arabic and Turkish). Yet there has been no large immigration wave from people from English-speaking countries into Belgium (in the recruitment process for the study children from international schools (cf. above) were excluded). Many of the families in the survey who used English at home held Belgian or other citizenships that are not traditionally connected with English. Anecdotal evidence also suggests that throughout Europe, many children from linguistically mixed couples without a connection to an English-speaking country overhear English at home through conversations between their parents and thus are exposed to English as a third first language. A fairly typical example here is a family in Flanders where the Italian mother spoke Italian to her young children, and the Belgian father used Dutch with them. The parents always spoke English to each other.

All across Europe, then, there are children growing up with English as an L1 at home, either as their only language, or as one of their two or more languages.

Children who do not have English as an L1 may start to learn English outside the home from an early age onwards. This is particularly the case in Great Britain and Ireland, where families with an immigration background often speak a language other than English at home (Carson 2010; Edwards 2001; see also the website of the (British) National Centre for Languages, http://www.cilt.org.uk/community_languages.aspx), and where children start to be addressed in English through day care or preschool. Li Wei (this volume) documents the early acquisition of English as a second language in Great Britain by three Chinese children in the second year of life. There are very few studies of Early Second Language Acquisition at this young age. Li Wei's study presents many different features of the early acquisition of English as an L2 and shows how in the early acquisition of grammar the children's English is influenced by their still developing Chinese. As such, Li Wei's study supports the view that contexts of acquisition should be fully taken into account in explanations of early bilingual development (see, e.g., De Houwer 1990, to appear), and that the acquisition of two languages from birth is a process that is substantially different from the very early acquisition of a second language after a first language has already started to develop.

The early acquisition of English as a second language in today's Europe is a process that is also more and more taking place outside of Great Britain and Ireland (see also Cenoz, this volume). Parents may buy media-based English language learning packages for their children such as the BBC's popular MUZZY program (see http://www.early-advantage.com/; MUZZY has not only been developed for English, but also for Brazilian Portuguese, French, German, Italian, Mandarin Chinese, Russian and Spanish). In many day care centers and preschools across Europe English may be introduced through songs and rhymes. It may also be offered through partial immersion, that is, through the fact that a childcare worker or preschool teacher addresses children exclusively in English for some of the time (Piske & Burmeister 2007; Wode 2006). As Cenoz (this volume) notes, though, there is a direct relation between the amount of exposure to a second language in the school context and the degree of proficiency one can expect in young learners. Often, the few hours per week that young children in English as a second language programs hear are simply not enough (ibid.).

More and more primary schools in Europe offer English as a first foreign language (Blondin, Candelier, Edelenbos, Johnstone, Kubanek-German & Taeschner 1998; see also Cenoz, this volume). Marjolijn Verspoor, Kees de Bot and Eva van Rein (this volume) note that the results of this pre-secondary English instruction are quite variable, with some pupils having a much higher degree of proficiency than others (cf. also Cenoz, this volume). Like Cenoz, Verspoor et al. emphasize the role of the amount of input. In a unique study, they compare the levels of English proficiency reached by a group of Dutch pupils with access to English through the media, and a group of Dutch pupils without such access. In addition, in each of these groups they distinguish between pupils who are in so-called 'bilingual education' tracks, which means they receive English-medium instruction about 50% of the time, and 'monolingual education' tracks, where English is restriced to a few hours' instruction per week.

Verspoor et al.'s findings show a clear influence of out-of-school media contact with English on pupils' developing English language proficiency. Cenoz (this volume) also emphasizes the role of exposure to English outside of school. European countries differ vastly from each other in the extent to which English is present in day-to-day life in general and in the media in particular (Berns, Claes, de Bot, Evers, Hasebrink, Huibregtse, Truchot & van der Wijst 2007). A major distinction can be made between countries or regions that use dubbing for originally English-speaking televsion programs and those that use subtitles (ibid.). With dubbing, no English is present. With subtitles, viewers get the original soundtrack, and, thus, they hear English.

The importance of subtitled English television programming as a particularly important context for foreign language learning is evidenced by a study of 353 Dutch-speaking children in Flanders (Kuppens & De Houwer 2006). The children were in the last year of primary school (aged 11 to 12) and had not had any English classes or personal contact with English speakers when they were tested. As part of several small tasks to test their English proficiency, children were asked to name anything they could see on a picture with many different things, people and actions on it. It turned out that more than half of the children could correctly name 16 or more objects, people or actions, and 10% were able to name over 40 (some even 85!). The more English television programs children watched, the higher their English proficiency.

Such findings, like the ones by Verspoor et al. (this volume), raise questions about the monolingual viewing experience that is so typical in larger European countries as France, Germany, Spain or Italy. If originally English-speaking children's programs were subtitled rather than dubbed, English teaching at school would get some much needed external support.

As Verspoor et al. (this volume) note, the level of proficiency targeted for English language teaching at the end of secondary school is B2 (according to the Common European Framework of Reference CEFR, Council of Europe 2001). This implies that when European students start higher education a level higher than B2 cannot be assumed. Yet, as Annelie Knapp notes in her chapter (this volume), more and more university courses in Europe are offered partly or entirely through English. A. Knapp shows that English-medium instruction (EMI) at German universities is not met with undivided enthusiasm and undertakes to investigate the benefits and potential problems that are involved in this specific use of English. Her conversational data from German university courses in chemistry reveal that interactional strategies characteristic of ELF (English as a Lingua Franca; see also Kohn, this volume and Seidlhofer, this volume) and native-nonnative discourse are less suitable in the EMI contexts. In everyday (ELF or native-nonnative) conversation, a considerable degree of vagueness and ambiguity can be tolerated and strategies are employed which focus on the continuation of the conversation rather than on attention to content (Long 1983). In academic discourse, however, "comprehension is crucial" (Knapp, this volume), affecting academic success, and researchers as well as decision makers in university education must take the specific conditions of EMI into account.

Even when competence in English is not an issue because all interlocutors involved have a very high command of the language, successful communication can be influenced and even threatened by cultural aspects. This point is taken up by Susan Gass and Daniel Reed (this volume) in their account of a cooperative project between Anatolia College in Greece and Michigan State University involving the development and implementation of an English testing procedure. Several cross-cultural problems arose during this enterprise that were not language related. Rather, the underlying cultural diversity and the particular culturally defined notions of the importance of testing were determining factors in how English and the testing of English were dealt with.

The chapters in this volume testify to the many different facets of English in a multilingual and multicultural Europe. They acknowledge the interdependence between cultures, languages and situations that influence and determine the use of English in Europe. It seems wise to move away from the common conception of unidirectional and powerful influence of English on linguistic diversity and cultural independence. Without English as a *lingua franca* there would be much less communication and mutual understanding amongst Europeans today. Let us embrace this language of wider communication and together with Europe's other languages make it our own.

References

Adams, J. N. 2003a. *Bilingualism and the Latin language*. Cambridge: CUP.

Adams, J. N. 2003b. Romanitas and the Latin language. *Classical Quarterly* 53: 184–205.

Adams, J. N. 2007. *The Regional Diversification of Latin 200BC–AD600*. Cambridge: CUP.

Baetens Beardsmore, H. 1993. The European School model. In *European Models of Bilingual Education*, H. Baetens Beardsmore (ed.), 121–154. Clevedon: Multilingual Matters.

Baugh, A. C. & Cable, T. 1978. *A History of the English Language*, 3rd edn. London: Routledge & Kegan Paul.

Berns, M., Claes, M. T., de Bot, K., Evers, R., Hasebrink, U., Huibregtse, I., Truchot, C. & van der Wijst, P. 2007. English in Europe. In *In the Presence of English. Media and European youth*, M. Berns, K. de Bot & U. Hasebrink (eds), 5–42. Berlin: Springer.

Blondin, C., Candelier, M., Edelenbos, P., Johnstone, R., Kubanek-German, A. & Taeschner, T. 1998. *Foreign Languages in Primary and Pre-school Education. A Review of Recent Research within the European Union*. London: CILT.

Cali, C., Stegu, M. & Vetter, E. 2008. Entretien avec Karlfried Knapp. *Synergies Europe* 3: 129–137.

Carli, A. & Ammon, U. (eds). 2008. *Linguistic Inequality in Scientific Communication Today* [*AILA Review* 20]. Amsterdam: John Benjamins.

Carson, L. 2010. Plurilingualism in Dublin: Immigrant languages at home and at school, Presentation at the 11th International CercleS Conference, 2–4 September 2010, Helsinki, Finland.

Caruana, S. 2007. Language use and attitudes in Malta. In *Multilingualism in European Bilingual Contexts. Language Use and Attitudes*, D. Lasagabaster & Á. Huguet (eds), 184–207. Clevedon: Multilingual Matters.

Hoby, T. (transl.) 1561/1967. *Hoby's Courtier of Castiglione*. New York NY: AMS.

Council of Europe. 2001. *Common European Framework of Reference for Languages: Learning, Teaching, Assessment*. Cambridge: CUP.

De Houwer, A. 1990. *The Acquisition of Two Languages from Birth*. Cambridge: CUP.

De Houwer, A. 2003. Home languages spoken in officially monolingual Flanders: A survey. *Plurilingua* 24: 71–87.

De Houwer, A. 2009a. *An Introduction to Bilingual Development*. Bristol: Multilingual Matters.

De Houwer, A. 2009b. *Bilingual First Language Acquisition*. Bristol: Multilingual Matters.

De Houwer, A. To appear. Learning environments and language development in bilingual acquisition. *Applied Linguistics Review*.

Deprez, C. 1995. *Les enfants bilingues: Langues et familles*. Paris: Didier.

Dürmüller, U. 1997. Territoriality and language freedom: The bridging and barrier function of the principles of territoriality and language freedom in multilingual Switzerland. In *Recent Studies in Contact Linguistics*, W. Wölck & A. De Houwer (eds), 92–100. Bonn: Dümmler.

Edwards, V. 2001. Community languages in the United Kingdom. In *The Other Languages of Europe*, G. Extra & D. Gorter (eds), 243–260. Clevedon: Multilingual Matters.

Ehlich, K. 2009. Modalitäten der Mehrsprachigkeit. *Zeitschrift für Angewandte Linguistik* 50: 7–31.

Extra, G. & Gorter, D. (eds). 2008. *Multilingual Europe. Facts and Policies*. Berlin: Mouton de Gruyter.

Extra, G. & Yagmur, K. (eds). 2004. *Urban Multilingualism in Europe: Immigrant Minority Languages at Home and School*. Clevedon: Multilingual Matters.

Extra, G. & Verhoeven, L. (eds). 1993. *Immigrant Languages in Europe*. Clevedon: Multilingual Matters.

Field, F. 2002. *Linguistic Borrowing in Bilingual Contexts* [Studies in Language Companion Series 62]. Amsterdam: John Benjamins.

Fishman, J. 2010. *European Vernacular Literary*. Bristol: Multilingual Matters.

Gardt, A. (ed.). 2000. *Nation und Sprache*. Berlin: de Gruyter.

Goebl, H., Nelde, P., Stary, Z. & Wölck, W. (eds). 1996. *Contact Linguistics. An International Handbook of Contemporary Research*, Vol. 2. Berlin: Walter de Gruyter.

Graddol, D. 2006. *English Next. Why Global English May Mean the End of English as a Foreign Language*. London: British Council.

Green, D. H. 1998. *Language and History in the Early Germanic World*. Cambridge: CUP.

Haye, T. 2005. *Lateinische Oralität*. Berlin: Walter de Gruyter.

House, J. 2008. English as lingua franca in Europe today. In *Multilingual Europe: Facts and Policies*, G. Extra & D. Gorter (eds), 63–85. Berlin: Mouton de Gruyter.

Karahan, F. 2005. Bilingualism in Turkey. In *ISB4: Proceedings of the 4th International Symposium on Bilingualism*, J. Cohen, K. T. McAlister, K. Rolstad & J. MacSwan, 1152–1166. Somerville MA: Cascadilla Press.

Kremnitz, G. 1990. *Gesellschaftliche Mehrsprachigkeit*. Wien: Braumüller.

Kuppens, A. & De Houwer, A. (eds). 2006. *De Relatie tussen Mediagebruik en Engelse Taalvaardigheid*. Antwerpen: Universiteit Antwerpen.

Lanza, E. & Svendsen, B. 2007. Tell me who your friends are and I might be able to tell you what language(s) you speak: Social network analysis and multilingualism. *International Journal of Bilingualism* 11: 275–300.

Long, M. 1983. Linguistic and conversational adjustments to non-native speakers. *Studies in Second Language Acquisition* 5: 177–193.

Maass, C. & Volmer, A. (eds). 2005. *Mehrsprachigkeit in der Renaissance*. Heidelberg: Universitätsverlag Winter.

Ministerium für Kultus, Jugend und Sport Baden-Württemberg (ed.). 2004. *Bildungsplan 2004. Allgemein bildendes Gymnasium*. <www.bildungsstandards-bw.de>.

Ó Riagáin, D. (ed.). 2006. *Voces Diversae: Lesser-Used Language Education in Europe*. Belfast: Cló Ollscoil na Banríona.

Pavlenko, A. 2006. Russian as a lingua franca. *Annual Review of Applied Linguistics* 26: 78–99.

Piske, T. & Burmeister, P. 2007. Erfahrungen mit früher englischer Immersion an norddeutschen Grundschulen. In *Aspekte bilingualen Lehrens und Lernens: Schwerpunkt Grundschule*, G. Schlemminger (ed.). Baltmannsweiler: Schneider-Verlag Hohengehren.

Quintilian, M. F. *Institutio Oratoria*. <http://www.thelatinlibrary.com/quintilian/quintilian.institutio1.shtml> (July 24, 2010).

Thomason, S. 2001. *Language Contact. An Introduction*. Washington DC: Georgetown University Press.

Wilton, A. 2009. Multilingualism and foreign language learning. In *Handbook of Foreign Languge Communication and Learning*, K. Knapp & B. Seidlhofer (eds), 45–78. Berlin: Mouton de Gruyter.

Wode, H. 2006. Mehrsprachigkeit durch immersive KiTas. Eine überzeugende Methode zum nachhaltigen Fremdsprachenerwerb. In *Zukunfts-Handbuch Kindertageseinrichtungen: Qualitätsmanagement für Träger, Leitung, Team*, H. Rieder-Aigner (ed.), 1–16. Regensburg: Walhalla. <www.fmks-online.de>.

Wright, R. 2004. Latin and English as world languages. *English Today* 20(4): 3–13.

The increasing role of English
in Basque education

Jasone Cenoz
University of the Basque Country, Spain

This paper focuses on the increasing role of English in the educational system of the Basque Autonomous Community in Spain. The position of English in the curriculum has become stronger in the last years and schools include multilingualism as one of their aims. This chapter discusses two main trends: first, the early introduction of English in pre-primary education when children are four years old or younger; second, the use of Content and Language Integrated Learning (CLIL) with English, along with Basque and Spanish as an additional medium of instruction. The paper also discusses studies aimed at examining the outcomes and effectiveness of these practices and the main challenges faced when teaching English in the Basque context.

1.   English in the Basque Country

English is the most important language of international communication both in Europe and elsewhere in the world. There have been languages of international communication in the past such as Latin or classical Arabic but the intensity of the use of English both geographically and affecting different domains is new (see Wilton & De Houwer this volume). English is considered a resource which opens doors for better opportunities and is associated with social and economic mobility. English has also reached the Basque Country but not to the same extent as in other European countries.

The spread of English is sometimes felt as a threat (see Nortier this volume). For example, Skutnabb-Kangas (2000) considers that English is a killer of other languages. Carli and Ammon (2008) focus on the disadvantages that scholars who are non-native speakers of English have in scientific publications and other aspects of academic life. The spread of English is seen as a reflection of globalization that in some cases can result in the loss of cultural identity. Some people feel that the influence of English is even more negative in the case of minority languages.

Others consider that English is only a threat if it replaces other languages in every-day communication but not when it is used as a *lingua franca* (Ferguson 2006).

English is becoming increasingly important for Basque citizens as a tool for communication both in Europe and in other parts of the world. In the Basque Autonomous Community (BAC) in Spain, English is considered a third language as is the case in other European bilingual areas such as Friesland, South Tyrol or Catalonia (Cenoz & Jessner 2000). In these areas, schools have at least three languages in the curriculum.

The spread of English in the world today is linked to its use along with other languages. As Graddol (2006) points out, this combination of English and other languages can be seen on the internet in the last years. English is still the most important language but the use of other languages on the internet has increased in the last years as well. The situation of "English and other languages" is common all over Europe with some exceptions in countries where English is the first language of the majority of the population. In the Basque Country, multilingualism with Basque, Spanish and English and even other languages is common in the linguistic landscape. This is particularly the case for international brand names. English is also used as part of a marketing strategy to communicate a feeling of modernity (Cenoz & Gorter 2006; see also Nortier this volume).

There are important differences between Northern and Southern European countries regarding the exposure to English in society and through the media. The Eurobarometer 243 (European Commission 2006) reports the results of a survey on language skills conducted with a sample of 28,694 subjects in the 27 EU countries, plus Croatia and Turkey. The results show that 56% of the sample can have a conversation in one or more languages other than their first language. The survey also indicates that English is the most common second or foreign language used and that 77% of EU citizens consider that children should learn English as their first foreign language at school. There is no specific data about the Basque Country in this survey but the ability to participate in a conversation in another language is relatively poor in Spain in general. According to Eurobarometer 237 (European Commission 2005), only 36% of the sample representing the Spanish population had skills in a second language and only 20% had skills in English. This is clearly different when compared to countries such as the Netherlands, Sweden or Denmark, where more than 80% of the population can hold a conversation in English.

Why do Spanish (and Basque) speakers have so many difficulties with English? Some of the reasons are the following:

– Lack of exposure in the social context. English is not used in everyday communication and there is very limited exposure to English in the media because of the policy of dubbing instead of using subtitles in the case of movies and TV. Even though there is potentially more contact with English because of internet and computer games, this exposure is still very limited because Spanish is a strong language even in these sectors.

- Linguistic distance. The phonological system of English is quite different from the Basque and Spanish phonological systems, particularly regarding the vowels, diphthongs and spelling. In general it is seen as difficult by Basque-Spanish speakers.
- Parents' knowledge of English. French used to be the main foreign language learned at school up to the 1980's and many parents do not speak English.
- Educational factors. In the past these factors included the use of out-dated or traditional instructional approaches, the lack of well-trained teachers with adequate proficiency in English, the large class sizes and the weak position of foreign languages in the school curriculum compared to subjects such as Mathematics or Spanish. Nowadays there is more attention to teacher education and the conditions for the teaching of English have improved, but these factors still play a role.

Acquiring proficiency in English is seen as necessary by many people in the Basque Country today. Parents realize that speaking English can be an advantage not only to find a job but also to have access to information and to interact with speakers of other languages. It is common for parents to take their children to language academies after school hours so that the children can take additional courses in English. In some cases it is because children need extra classes in order to pass the school exams and in others it is because parents just want their children to learn more English. Teachers in these language academies are in many cases native speakers of English and they prepare children for specific certificates. An additional source of exposure are summer courses in English speaking countries.

2.   English in education in the Basque Country

English has become more important in the school curriculum in recent years and schools include multilingualism as one of their aims. In the last two decades there has been an important shift in emphasis from French to English and, at present, English is studied as a foreign language by over 95% of Basque school children. Thus, the Basque Country has followed the same trend as the rest of Spain and much of Europe, where English is the first foreign language at school. French (and exceptionally German) is another foreign language used at school in the Basque Country but it is usually learned as a fourth language.

In spite of this, exposure to English outside of school is still very limited and most teachers and parents do not speak English because they learned French at school. The situation is changing with the new generations. There are no studies of teachers' proficiency in English but it seems that it is not very high among primary school teachers (Cenoz 2009). In general, secondary school teachers of English have a high level of English proficiency because most of them have a degree in English Studies and studied many courses (mainly literature and linguistics) through the medium of English. Primary school teachers have more training in psychology and pedagogy but nowadays there are a growing number of teachers who have had specific training as teachers of English. Both in primary and secondary school it is still often the case that only teachers of English speak English. The rest of the teachers do not speak English as it is the case for the majority of the population in Spain.

With very few exceptions, teachers of English in the Basque Country are native speakers of Basque or Spanish both in public and private schools. There are a few French, English and German schools where these foreign languages are taught as subjects and languages of instruction. Some of the school children attending these schools are speakers of the foreign languages who live in the Basque Country but many others are local students. The number of native teachers is higher in these international schools.

The conditions for learning English at school have improved in the last years and both the Basque Government and other organizations have made a great effort to reinforce and improve the teaching of English. The actions carried out in the last years include subsidizing intensive language learning courses for English teachers both in the Basque Country and abroad and important changes in the teaching methods. Nowadays the acquisition of oral skills has become a priority in some classes, especially in pre-primary and primary school. In many cases the materials for the teaching of English include new technologies and have been created by teacher trainers and teachers to be experimented with in the schools. The general policy is not to mix English with other languages. Teachers are supposed to use only English in class. With the exception of dictionaries, teaching materials are in English only.

English is a third language in Basque schools where Basque and Spanish are either first or second languages and are used as school subjects and languages of instruction. The increasing importance of English in the curriculum has had an influence on the whole educational system that is moving from bilingual to multilingual education. The interest in multilingual education is also reflected in the conferences organized on this topic in the last years to discuss the Basque situation as compared to other examples of bilingual and multilingual education. Some examples of these activities are the seven conferences organized by the Gaztelueta

Foundation (http://www.jornadasgaztelueta.org) or the six conferences organized by Getxoko Berritzegune (http://www.getxolinguae.net/). The Basque Government Department of Education supports the development of trilingual education and subsidizes different activities such as courses, seminars and projects.

Although most schools still draw clear boundaries between the languages in the curriculum (Basque, Spanish, English and French as an optional subject), there is also a trend towards integrated curricula. In schools with integrated curricula, teachers of the three or four languages work together when planning their classes so that the contents and the different skills used in the language classes are related to each other (Arano, Berazadi & Idiazabal 1996; Mugertza & Aliaga 2005). The idea of an integrated curriculum including different languages can provide an opportunity towards developing metalinguistic awareness and benefiting from multilingualism (see also Jessner 2008). As Elorza and Muñoa (2008) explain, an integrated curriculum offers the opportunity for comparing specific aspects of the different languages and "at the same time it transfers, applies and generalizes what has been learned in one language to the others" (Elorza & Muñoa 2008:91).

Specific projects meant for increasing the role of English in the curriculum started in the 1990's. The most popular project has been the early learning of English from the second year of pre-primary education onwards (age 4). Other projects involve the use of a Content and Language Integrated Learning (CLIL) approach in the English language classes or when English is used as an additional language of instruction. These projects will be discussed in more detail in the following sections.

Parents support these projects because they are aware of the need to improve the level of communicative skills in English. According to a study conducted by the Basque Institute of Educational Evaluation and Research, parents believe that it is important for their children to learn several languages. They also think that English is useful for travelling and for getting to know people and countries as well as for the job market (ISEI-IVEI 2007).

3.   Early learning of English

One of the consequences of the need to acquire higher levels of proficiency in English is the trend towards the introduction of English in pre-primary or primary school in several European countries (Eurydice 2008). A recent initiative towards the reinforcing of early foreign language learning is the Piccolingo campaign launched by the European Commission in September 2009 (http://www.piccolingo.eu/). This campaign is aimed at parents in order to raise their awareness of the advantages of acquiring foreign languages from an early age.

According to the Piccolingo campaign children who have early contact with a foreign language will:

- find communication easier
- learn and memorize through play
- be well-prepared for school
- learn to be open-minded
- feel at home in any country
- increase their chances of finding a job
- find foreign cultures attractive rather than threatening
- appreciate their own culture.

Nowadays, 90% of the schools in the Basque Autonomous Community teach English from the age of four, although it is not compulsory until the age of six. This very early introduction of English has also taken place in some areas in Spain but it is not as common in other parts of Europe. The early learning of English in pre-school started in the Basque Country almost 20 years ago. The first project to introduce English as a school subject in pre-school was called *Eleanitz Proiektua* (Multilingualism Project) and started in several Basque-medium schools (*ikastolak*) in 1991. In these schools, English started being taught to children aged 4 years for two hours a week in four 30-minute sessions. The project soon spread to many other schools. In 1996 the Basque Government Department of Education selected a number of schools and allowed them to choose among the following possibilities: (1) the introduction of English in pre-primary school at the age of four for two or three hours a week; (2) the introduction of English in the third year of primary school (at the age of 8) but with an increased frequency of exposure, i.e., five hours a week and using a content-based approach; (3) the introduction of English in the third year of primary school with later on five hours of English per week in secondary school using a content based approach. The early learning of English was already so popular by 1996 that most schools implemented the early introduction of English at the pre-school level. Thus, a comparative evaluation of the three possibilities was not possible.

Most children in the BAC start attending school at the age of two. The classrooms are equipped for the needs of these young children and the school day is shorter. The language that children start out with at school frequently is Basque, which is their first or second language. English is introduced in the second or third year of pre-primary school when children are 3 to 4 years old and have already been exposed to Basque. The schools participating in the different programs for the early introduction of English receive support from the teachers' guidance units so they can get access to materials for the classroom and learn how to use them. The English language teachers participating in these programs only use English in the classroom and all the activities are oral. The methodology used is based on story-telling, songs and other oral activities and requires the children's active participation by means of collective dramatization and playing.

One of the main reasons for the early introduction of English in the Basque Country is the pressure from parents who want their children to learn English and who think that an early introduction necessarily results in a higher level of competence. Before the early introduction of English spread to the whole system, individual schools had an interest in offering something 'special' because they needed to attract students in a social context in which the birth rate is very low. Introducing English at an early age has some difficulties but can be easier to organize than other ways to increase exposure to English in later years when there is more pressure to make sure there is enough time for all the school subjects so as to meet the required standards.

In general the attitudes of teachers and parents towards the early learning of English are very positive (Cenoz 2009). The early introduction of English has spread all over the BAC but it has also been criticized. Some have suggested that the increasing role of English in the curriculum could be an obstacle for the revitalization of the Basque language (Etxeberria 2002, 2004; Ruiz Bikandi 2005). The hours devoted to English are hours that in many schools were previously taught in Basque. Others see English as just a hype. Another criticism is that there are not enough qualified teachers and that the money spent in teacher education and material development should be used for other purposes.

Several research studies carried out in the Basque Country have focused on the effect of the early learning of English on the development of different aspects of English proficiency (see Garcia Mayo & Garcia Lecumberri 2003; Cenoz 2009). Taking into account that there may be an interaction between age and variables such as the amount of exposure, cognitive development or teaching methodology, two different methodological designs have been used. Some studies have controlled for the age of testing (Type A) and others for the number of hours of instruction (Type B).

Type A studies analyze whether learners who are the same age but have had different amounts of exposure achieve the same level of proficiency in English. The advantage of this approach is that all learners are the same age at the time of testing. However, it is difficult to isolate the age factor from the effect of exposure because in the case of Basque schools, early learners have had more hours of exposure to the language than late learners. Cenoz (2009) carried out a comparison in the 6th year of primary school. Participants were school children who had started learning English either in pre-primary (age 4) or in primary school (age 8). They completed a background questionnaire, a cloze test and two oral production tests. At the time of testing, subjects who had started learning

English at the age of 4 had received approximately 700 hours of instruction and subjects who had started learning English at the age of 8 had received 400 hours of instruction. The results of the comparison between the two groups were very mixed. For one of the written tests, the cloze test, learners who started their English classes at the age of 8 obtained significantly better results than learners who started at the age of 4. Significant differences were also found in pronunciation and vocabulary but contrary to the predictions, the scores obtained by the learners who started at the age of 8 (400 hours of exposure) were significantly *higher* than the scores on these two measures obtained by the subjects who started at the age of 4 (700 hours of exposure). There were no significant differences between the two groups for the grammar, fluency and content scores in the oral production tests. Other measures of oral proficiency such as the number of lexical tokens and lexical types also showed differences but in this case early learners obtained higher scores. These combined findings, then, do not show a clear positive effect of the early introduction of English. There is no clear pattern showing advantages on part of the learners who have received more hours of instruction.

Similar results were obtained in two other type A studies that looked at English proficiency at the same age of testing but with children who had different amounts of exposure. Ruiz de Zarobe (2006) made a comparison using a sample of respondents with the same characteristics regarding year of testing (6th year of primary school), hours of instruction (400 vs. 700) and age of introduction of English (4 vs. 8). She focused on the use of the negative (*no/not*; aux. + *not*; aux. + *n't)* in oral production during a story telling task. She found that in general terms the acquisition of the negative was at a very early stage for both groups because they were still at the stage of inserting "no/not" rather than using auxiliary full and contracted forms. Ruiz de Zarobe did not find any significant differences between the two groups even though participants who had started learning English at the age of 4 had had 300 hours more of exposure to English than children who had started learning English at 8.

Egiguren (2006) compared students who had started taking English classes at pre-primary school when they were 4 years old to students who had started in the 3rd year of primary school when they were 8 years old. The comparison was carried out in the 4th year of primary school, that is, when the early learners were in their 5th year of English and the late learners in their 2nd year. The early learners had had three hours of English per week and the late learners four: two actual English classes and two art classes taught through the medium of English. Egiguren tested vocabulary, listening comprehension, reading and writing skills in English and found no differences between the two groups. Different results were reported by Garagorri (2002) in the 2nd year of secondary school. He found differences in favor of early learners for writing, reading, listening comprehension, speaking and grammar. These results are much more positive for early learners than reported in any of the other studies. One possible explanation could be methodological and have to do with the type of test: Egiguren used standardized tests, which were not used in the other studies.

Type B studies compared proficiency in English for learners who had the same number of hours of exposure but who started learning English at different ages. The advantage of this approach is that all learners have the same number of hours of instruction, but its weakness is that learners are not the same age at the time of testing. Differences between learners could thus either be due to the age factor but also to differences in cognitive maturity and test-taking strategies.

Type B studies have looked at general proficiency, phonetics, writing and specific aspects of morphology and syntax (see Garcia Mayo & Garcia Lecumberri 2003; Ruiz Zarobe 2005; Lasagabaster & Doiz 2003 and Cenoz 2009, for reviews). The comparisons were carried out at different stages when learners had had between 400 and 800 hours of English. The results clearly indicate that older learners progress faster or at least are able to show their progress in the tests better than younger learners when the amount of instruction is controlled for. Specific studies on phonetics (García Lecumberri & Gallardo 2003, 2006) similarly fail to show any advantages for early exposure to English. The differences are more pronounced for those measures related to metalinguistic ability than for quantitative measures of oral production or pronunciation. This could be due to cognitive maturity and also to the methodological approach used with older learners, which was more traditional and grammar oriented.

The combined results of type A and type B studies fail to show that introducing English at pre-primary school levels leads to higher levels of English proficiency. Any advantages on the part of early learners are limited to a few specific areas in type A studies for those early learners who received more hours of instruction. Learners who have been exposed to English since the age of 4 have the possibility of having more hours of exposure to English than learners who start learning English four years later, but the results do not provide clear evidence that supports the early introduction of English as the most efficient way for learning the language. Even when English is introduced in kindergarten, exposure is limited, since there is no opportunity for hearing or using the language outside school. Because the level of English proficiency achieved through school, including through the early introduction of English, is often not considered high enough, many Basque children try to make up for the limited nature of English language exposure by attending after-school English evening classes and summer courses in English speaking countries.

4.   CLIL and using English as an additional language of instruction

CLIL or Content and Language Integrated Learning includes a wide range of teaching practices but its main characteristic is that it focuses on the acquisition of language-independent concepts and skills as well as an additional language at the same time (see also Marsh 2007; Dalton-Puffer 2007). CLIL "is a dual-focused educational approach in which an additional language is used for the learning and teaching of both content and language" (Marsh, in press). Both language and content are equally important in CLIL. Content from different academic disciplines is taught at the same time as the target language. For instance, social sciences, music, science or mathematics are taught through the target language using language-supportive methodologies.

CLIL enjoys strong support from European institutions and can develop in different ways depending on the context in which it is used (Coyle 2007). It is difficult, however, to establish clear boundaries between CLIL and other content-based approaches developed outside Europe (see Met 1998; Carrasquillo & Rodriguez 2002). CLIL is also close to some types of immersion programs. One of the characteristics of CLIL is its origin in foreign language teaching and not in bilingual education. These two areas have traditionally ignored each other. The "foreign language" perspective can be seen when Seikkula-Leiono (2007) discusses the differences between immersion and CLIL and points out that in immersion reading and writing are taught in the second language whereas in CLIL they are taught in the first language. Apart from this clear difference, which, however, may not even apply to all types of CLIL, the other points of comparison that Seikkula-Leiono (2007) lists are not always so different in practice because there are many types of immersion programs in bilingual education and many types of CLIL. Both in immersion and CLIL, previous knowledge of the L2 may be present, teachers may be fluent bilinguals and there may be differences in exposure to the target language in the school curriculum.

Following the trend in other European areas (Eurydice 2008), CLIL has had an important influence on the teaching of English. In 1996 the Basque Government Department of Education introduced a content-based approach in some primary schools. Nowadays, approximately 25% of the primary schools in the Basque Country (serving about 20,000 students) and 9% of secondary schools (serving about 1600 students) are 'officially' participating in a special CLIL project but many other schools also use a CLIL approach to teaching English as a third language.

The Basque Country has a long tradition of bilingual education through immersion. For instance, immersion takes place in the case of speakers of Spanish as a first language who have Basque as the medium of instruction. However, the integration of content and language is not as explicit in these programs as in the case of CLIL. Spanish L1 learners in Basque-medium education have school subjects such as mathematics and science through the medium of Basque. In addition, they have Basque language classes. Compared to CLIL, Basque-medium bilingual programs establish much more of a formal separation between the "content subjects" and "language classes", although in practice language can also be the focus of attention in content subjects. At the same time, some type of content such as literature is often taught as part of the Basque language classes.

In the case of English classes 'officially' using a CLIL approach two possibilities exist. In some cases, traditional English language classes are replaced by CLIL classes so that the teacher of English uses a content-based approach in the English language classes including topics from different subjects: geography, history, music, mathematics, etc. In other cases, teachers who are proficient in English use English as the language of instruction for teaching a particular subject. These teachers are thus teachers of the content subjects rather than English teachers. The choice of one or the other option depends on the availability of teachers who can speak English. In both cases there is support for teachers. Materials are often designed by teacher trainers and consultants who also organize regular meetings with teachers and visit the classes. Schools participating in CLIL projects get special funding. The selection of the content to be taught through the medium of English depends on different factors such as the school grade and the specific language skills needed to be able to follow the classes.

The use of a CLIL approach in English classes and the early learning of English may have limited results when instruction through English only takes place three or four hours per week at school and English exposure is almost non-existent outside of school. Some schools have decided to use English as the language of instruction at the end of primary school and in secondary school (Cenoz 2009). Using English as an additional language of instruction is more complex than the early introduction of English in pre-primary school or the use of a CLIL approach in English language classes. It implies readjustments for teaching staff because of the distribution of the language of instruction over different subjects. There are also some challenges regarding the teaching materials because students need to learn the same content regardless of whether a subject is taught through the medium of English or through Basque and Spanish. This means that many materials that are available in English need to be adapted. In some cases the Basque or Spanish materials are translated into English. In many cases there are problems in finding specialized teachers who can teach subjects through the medium of English.

In spite of these difficulties some schools are using English as the medium of instruction. In most cases this is a follow-up to the early introduction of English in pre-primary school and the CLIL approach in the English classes. Some of these schools have Basque as the language of instruction, Spanish as a school subject and English then becomes an additional language of instruction for a few subjects. In other cases, Basque and Spanish are the languages of instruction and English is added as an additional language of instruction.

The subjects taught through the medium of English may be social sciences, natural science, arts, music, computer science, handicrafts, religion or chemistry. The choice of the different subjects and the levels at which to teach through the medium of English depend on the school's organization and the availability of teachers in the schools. With a few exceptions, teachers have Basque or Spanish as a first language but there is a policy of "one person-one language" so that teachers who teach English or in English use English in their classes and do not teach in the other two languages. The use of English as an additional language of instruction can also be considered a more intensive CLIL approach and in this case it is not clearly distinguishable from immersion programs in bilingual education.

Some research studies have looked at the effect of using English as an additional language of instruction on learners' English proficiency. These studies draw comparisons between experimental and control groups. All the students are studying English as a subject but students in the experimental groups have more exposure to English because English is also the language of instruction for an additional subject. Studies have looked at specific aspects of English language proficiency such as phonetics, vocabulary, morphology and syntax (see Gallardo, Gómez Lacabex & García Lecumberri 2009; Jiménez Catalán & Ruiz de Zarobe 2009; Villarreal & García Mayo 2009 or Martínez Adrián & Gutiérrez 2009). The results indicate that students with English both as a subject and as an additional language of instruction obtain higher scores than students who only study English as a subject. These results do not, however, necessarily prove the positive effect of CLIL, since there are substantial differences in the amount of instruction. Students in the CLIL programs had the regular English language classes plus a subject through the medium of English and that accounted for 300 hours more of exposure to English than the non-CLIL students. The results prove that more exposure to English by using English as the medium of instruction to teach a school subject produces better results, but it is not clear whether these results could have been obtained by just increasing the number of English language classes.

A study carried out by the Ikastolak network has confirmed the effect of the amount of exposure. As expected, students in a CLIL program with English as the language of instruction for Social Sciences who also had regular English language classes did better in English than students who only learned English in their regular English language classes (Ikastolen Elkarteko Eleanitz-Ingelesa Taldea 2003). This study also looked at achievement in Social Sciences and showed that students with English as the language of instruction obtained similar or even more positive results than the control group.

The use of English as a language of instruction has also reached the universities in the Basque Country. The need to have the necessary skills in English in order to access scientific information and to communicate with students and researchers from other countries is increasing and Basque universities are becoming aware of this need. For example, the University of the Basque Country has promoted the use of Basque as the language of instruction and it is now adding instruction through English. The Multilingualism Plan, which started in 2005, has four aims: (1) to foster mobility and participation in the European Higher Education Area (EHEA); (2) to follow up on the multilingualism projects developed at secondary school; (3) to foster the mobility of teaching staff, and (4) to better prepare students for the labor market. The number of courses at the undergraduate level taught through the medium of English is over 100. This is a small figure compared to the total number of courses, but the number is increasing every year. There are, in addition, some courses at the graduate level that are taught through English or French.

5.   Future perspectives

The early introduction of second and foreign languages has attracted the interest of parents, schools and politicians across Europe. Learning a second or foreign language from an early age may have cultural and social advantages but it is important to keep in mind that if exposure is limited to a few hours of contact with the target language in the school context the results in terms of proficiency may be also limited (García Mayo & García Lecumberri 2003; Muñoz 2006a; Cenoz 2009). Some studies prove that young children can achieve a higher level of proficiency than older children but this is generally only the case when there is massive exposure to the target language both at school and outside of school (see Singleton & Ryan 2004; Muñoz 2006b, for a review).

The early introduction of English at school has a relatively long tradition in the Basque Country. However, experience with the early learning of Basque in pre-primary education for Spanish speaking children has an even longer history. Children who have Spanish as their first language and Spanish as the language of instruction have classes in Basque starting in pre-primary school all the way to the end of secondary school. The results of evaluations show the limitations of having Basque classes just for a few hours per week as compared to having Basque not only as a school subject but also as the language of instruction (see Cenoz 2009 for a review). Now that the early learning of foreign languages is being promoted, it is important for researchers and language planners to take into consideration the experience of learning a minority language as a second language from a very early age. The use of a minority language as the language of instruction for speakers of the majority language is also well documented in Catalonia, Ireland, Wales and Friesland (Harris 2008; Lewis 2008; Gorter & van der Meer 2008; Vila i Moreno 2008). Research conducted on second language learning in bilingual education programs can certainly provide interesting information for foreign language learning as well (Cenoz & Gorter 2008). Obviously, bilingual education research could also benefit from findings in foreign language acquisition.

The increasing role of English in Basque education shows a trend also found in other parts of Europe. English is getting more space in the school curriculum. More research is needed, however, to try to identify the most efficient ways for learning English that take into account the role of age, frequency of language exposure and teaching methods.

Acknowledgment

This chapter has been written with the assistance of the research grant EDU2009-11601 from the Spanish Ministry of Science and Technology and the Basque Government funding for the research group "Donostia Research on Education and Multilingualism (DREAM)".

References

Arano, R. M., Berazadi, E. & Idiazabal, I. 1996. Planteamiento discursivo e integrador de un proyecto de educación trilingüe. In *Las Lenguas en la Europa comunitaria*. Vol. II, M. Pujol & F. Sierra (eds), 65–88. Amsterdam: Rodopi.

Carli, A. & Ammon, U. (eds). 2008. Linguistic inequality in scientific communication today. *Aila Review* 20 (special issue).

Carrasquillo, A. L. & Rodriguez, V. 2002. *Language Minority Students in the Mainstream Classroom*. Clevedon: Multilingual Matters.

Cenoz, J. 2009. *Towards Multilingual Education: Basque Educational Research in International Perspective*. Bristol: Multilingual Matters.

Cenoz, J. & Jessner, U. (eds). 2000. *English in Europe: The Acquisition of a Third Language*. Clevedon: Multilingual Matters.

Cenoz, J. & Gorter, D. 2006. Linguistic landscape and minority languages, *The International Journal of Multilingualism* 3: 67–80.

Cenoz, J. & Gorter, D. 2008. Applied linguistics and the use of minority languages in education. *Aila Review* 21: 1–12.

Coyle, D. 2007. CLIL – A pedagogical approach from the European perspective. In *Encyclopedia of Language and Education*, Vol 4: *Second and Foreign Language Education*, N. van Deussen-Scholl & N. Hornberger (eds), 97–111. Berlin: Springer.

Dalton-Puffer, C. 2007. *Discourse in Content and Language Integrated Learning (CLIL) Classrooms* [Language Learning & Language Teaching 20]. Amsterdam: John Benjamins.

Ferguson, G. 2006. *Language Planning and Education*. Edinburgh: EUP.

Egiguren, I. 2006. Atzerriko hizkuntza goiztiarraren eragina gaitasun eleaniztunean. PhD dissertation, University of the Basque Country.

Elorza, I. & Muñoa, I. 2008. Promoting the minority language through integrated plurilingual language planning: the case of the ikastolas. *Language, Culture and Curriculum* 21: 85–101.

Etxeberria, F. 2002. Educación trilingüe precoz en el País Vasco y la bicicleta de Cummins. In *¿Trilingües a los 4 años?*, F. Etxeberria & U. Ruiz Bikandi (eds), 165–191. Donostia: Ibaeta Pedagogía.

Etxeberria, F. 2004. Trilinguals at four? Early trilingual education in the Basque Country. In *Trilingualism in Family, School and Community*, C. Hoffmann & J. Ytsma (eds), 185–201. Clevedon: Multilingual Matters.

European Commission. 2005. *Eurobarometer 237: Europeans and languages*. <http://ec.europa. eu/public_opinion/archives/ebs/ebs_237.en.pdf>.

European Commission. 2006. *Eurobarometer 243. Europeans and their languages*. <http:// ec.europa.eu/public_opinion/archives/ebs/ebs_243_sum_en.pdf>.

Eurydice. 2008. *Key Data on Teaching Languages at School in Europe*. <http://eacea.ec.europa. eu/ressources/eurydice/pdf/0_integral/095EN.pdf>.

Gallardo, F., Gómez Lacabex, E. & García Lecumberri, M. L. 2009. Testing the effectiveness of content and language integrated learning in foreign language contexts. In *Content and Language Integrated Learning*, Y. Ruiz de Zarobe & R. Jiménez Catalán (eds), 63–80. Bristol: Multilingual Matters.

Garagorri, X. 2002. Hirueletasun goiztiarra ikastoletan "Eleanitz-Ingelesa" proiektuaren ebaluazioa. In *¿Trilingües a los 4 años?*, F. Etxeberria & U. Ruiz Bikandi (eds), 105–143. Donostia: Ibaeta Pedagogía.

García Mayo, M. P. & García Lecumberri, M. L. (eds). 2003. *Age and the Acquisition of English as a Foreign Language*. Clevedon: Multilingual Matters.

García Lecumberri M. L. & Gallardo, F. 2003. English FL sounds in school learners of different ages. In *Age and the Acquisition of English as a Foreign Language*, M. P. García Mayo & M. L. García Lecumberri (eds), 115–135. Clevedon: Multilingual Matters.

García Lecumberri M. L. & Gallardo, F. 2006. Ingelezko bokalen pertzepzioa eta ekoizpena atzerriko hizkuntza gisa: Jatorrizko kategoria fonetikoen eta hasteko adinaren eragina. In *Hizkuntzak Ikasten eta Erabiltzen*, J. Cenoz & D. Lasagabaster (eds), 159–175. Bilbo: Euskal Herriko Unibertsitatea.

Gorter, D. & van der Meer, C. 2008. Developments in bilingual Frisian-Dutch education in Friesland. *Aila Review* 21: 87–103.

Graddol, D. 2006. *English next. Why Global English may mean the end of English as a Foreign language*. London: British Council.

Harris, J. 2008. The declining role of primary schools in the revitalisation of Irish. *Aila Review* 21: 49–68.

Ikastolen Elkarteko Eleanitz-ingelesa taldea. 2003. Eleanitz-English: Gizarte Zientziak ingelesez. *Bat Soziolinguistika Aldizkaria* 49: 79–97.

ISEI-IVEI. 2007. Research on trilingual students in secondary school. Bilbao: ISEI-IVEI.

Jessner, U. 2008. A DST model of multilingualism and the role of metalinguistic awareness. *Modern Language Journal* 92: 270–283.

Jiménez Catalán, R. & Ruiz de Zarobe, Y. 2009. The receptive vocabulary of EFL learners in two instructional contexts: CLIL versus non-CLIL instruction. In *Content and Language Integrated Learning*, Y. Ruiz de Zarobe & R. Jiménez Catalán (eds), 81–92. Bristol: Multilingual Matters.

Lasagabaster, D. & Doiz, A. 2003. Maturational constraints on foreign-language written production. In *Age and the Acquisition of English as a Foreign Language*, M. P. García Mayo & M. L. García Lecumberri (eds), 136–160. Clevedon: Multilingual Matters.

Lewis, G. 2008. Current challenges in bilingual education in Wales. *Aila Review* 21: 69–86.

Marsh, C. 2007. Language Awareness and CLIL. In *Encyclopedia of Language and Education*, Vol 6: *Knowledge about Language*, J. Cenoz & N. Hornberger (eds), 233–246. New York NY: Springer.

Marsh, D. In press. Content and language integrated learning. *The Wiley-Blackwell Encyclopedia of Applied Linguistics*. London: Blackwell.

Martínez Adrián, M. & Gutiérrez, J. 2009. The acquisition of English syntax by CLIL learners in the Basque Country. In *Content and Language Integrated Learning*, Y. Ruiz de Zarobe & R. Jiménez Catalán (eds), 176–196. Bristol: Multilingual Matters.

Met, M. 1998. Curriculum decision-making in content-based language teaching. In *Beyond Bilingualism: Multilingualism and Multilingual Education*, J. Cenoz & F. Genesee (eds), 35–63. Clevedon: Multilingual Matters.

Mugertza, K. & Aliaga, R. 2005. El multilingüismo y el multiculturalismo en el sistema educativo vasco. In *Multilingüismo y Multiculturalismo en la Escuela*, D. Lasagabaster & J. M. Sierras (eds), 97–112. Barcelona: ICE/ Horsori.

Muñoz, C. (ed.). 2006a. *Age and the Rate of Foreign Language Learning*. Clevedon: Multilingual Matters.

Muñoz, C. 2006b. The effects of age on foreign language learning: The BAF Project. In *Age and the Rate of Foreign Language Learning*, C. Muñoz (ed.), 1–40. Clevedon: Multilingual Matters.

Ruiz Bikandi, U. 2005. La reflexió interlingüística: Ajudar a pensar en/amb/sobre tres llengües. *Articles de Didàctica de la Llengua i de la Literatura* 38: 51–66.

Ruiz de Zarobe, Y. 2005. Age and third language production: A longitudinal study. *International Journal of Multilingualism* 2: 105–112.

Ruiz de Zarobe, Y. 2006. Garapen kognitiboa eta adina ingelesaren jabekuntzan atzerriko hizkuntza gisa. In *Hizkuntzak Ikasten eta Erabiltzen*, J. Cenoz & D. Lasagabaster (eds), 177–191. Bilbo: Euskal Herriko Unibertsitatea.

Seikkula-Leiono, J. 2007. CLIL learning: Achievement levels and affective factors. *Language and Education* 21: 328–341.

Singleton, D. & Ryan, L. 2004. *Language Acquisition: The Age Factor*. Clevedon: Multilingual Matters.

Skutnabb-Kangas, T. 2000. *Linguistic Genocide in Education or Worldwide Diversity and Human Rights?* Mahwah NJ: Lawrence Erlbaum Associates.

Vila i Moreno, F. X. 2008. Language-in-education policies in the Catalan language area. *Aila Review* 21: 31–48.

Villarreal, I. & García Mayo, M. P. 2009. Tense and agreement morphology in the interlanguage of Basque/Spanish bilinguals: CLIL versus non-CLIL. In *Content and Language Integrated Learning*, Y. Ruiz de Zarobe & R. Jiménez Catalán (eds), 157–175. Bristol: Multilingual Matters.

English language testing

A case study of test development in Greece

Susan M. Gass and Daniel Reed
Michigan State University, USA

This paper chronicles the development of an English language test in Greece. The observations include data from surveys of school owners, instructors, Greek test item reviewers, students, and parents. The focus in the analysis is on how both the internal (psychometric and content) characteristics of the test and the circumstances surrounding its commission and use reflect major changes in the role that English is playing in the Greek context. The results show the importance of a complete understanding of the cultural context. We point out how intercultural sensitivities play out and can potentially derail a project such as the one described in this paper if intercultural issues are not adequately addressed.

Introduction

The increasing importance of English in Europe is indisputable. Numerous accounts of its function have been discussed in the recent past, including its role as a *lingua franca* (Seidlhofer, Breiteneder & Pitzl 2006; Knapp & Meierkord 2002; Meierkord & Knapp 2002) as well as its role as an integrative force (Phillipson 2003). Alongside the growing need in Europe to know English for daily, political or business purposes is the need to assess the knowledge and abilities that individuals have. This paper describes the context of English-language testing in one European country, namely Greece. We chronicle the experiences of one U.S.-based university, Michigan State University, through the long process of test development (including initial contact and development of a team), attempts at understanding the target culture, test piloting (including a focus on test appearance as well as on test content), gaining approval within Greece, and finally the test launch. Throughout, we emphasize the cross-cultural differences that at times hampered our progress.

Background

In Greece, knowledge of English is considered important if one is to gain access to certain prestigious professions as well as to gain access to a variety of educational opportunities (Tsagari 2009). Given the importance of English in Greek society, it is somewhat surprising that there has not been large-scale reform within the school system with regard to English language teaching. Because the school system is not able to keep up with societal demands, parents frequently turn to private language schools for further language education and enroll their children in *frontistiria*, which are well-respected privately-owned institutions that teach English as well as other languages. According to Tsagari (2009), in 1995, there were more than 7000 frontistiria in Greece with enrollments of over 1,000,000.

To support the emphasis on English language teaching, English language testing has become a significant industry in Greece, as is evidenced by the number of commercial and university-based tests vying for a market share. Important in the history of tests in Europe, and, by extension in Greece, was the Council of Europe's development of the Common European Framework of Reference for Languages (CEFR). The goal of this project was to develop a common, descriptive system for use in the development of curricular guidelines, syllabi, textbooks and examinations, and in the communicating of ability levels for a variety of purposes for all languages of Europe (Council of Europe 2001). The CEFR system includes a set of common reference levels for language development. This system is comprised of three main categories (A – basic user, B – independent user, and C – proficient user) and two divisions within each of those categories (i.e., A1, A2, B1, B2, C1, C2).

It is important to point out at this juncture that government-approved examinations are necessary for a range of positions, including civil service positions and positions in the tourist industry. In order to have an examination approved by the Greek government, external bodies must apply to ASEP (ΑΣΕΠ – Civil Service Staffing Council) for official recognition. As the current project developed, the application to ASEP which we describe in greater detail below, turned out to be a major part of the entire process. The path toward approval turned out to be somewhat lengthy, confusing, and, at times, complex.

To date there are 14 ASEP-approved examinations that are administered in Greece for the B2 level and 11 for the C2 level. In 1970 the University of Cambridge's First Certificate in English (FCE) examination (aligned to the B2 level of the Common European Framework of Reference) became the first test to enter the Greek market. The other large test in Greece is administered by the University of Michigan; their C2 equivalent examination has been in existence for more than 25 years, while their lower-level (B2) examination was first administered in 1994. To underscore the Greek emphasis on the FCE and by implication high-stakes tests of English in Greece, Tsagari (2009) points out that in 1995, there were 246,717 candidates world-wide who took the FCE examination (Cambridge) and of those, 115,279 were in Greece. Thus, the Greek market represented nearly 47% of the total world-wide FCE testing population in 1995. In addition, Tsagari reports that the Greek test-takers (data from 1994) were approximately 15 years old. The general average age of the FCE population as a whole, however, is 22 years old. The second largest test is the test developed by the University of Michigan, for which the Greek market represents 90% of their entire testing operation (letter of January 17, 2007 from Presidents of two Greek colleges). In other words, English language testing in Greece is pervasive and starts at a very young age, much younger than in other parts of the world. This became known to us as the "Greek certificate culture".

Accompanying the commercial tests are numerous books that prepare students for particular tests, for example, the University of Michigan and the Cambridge tests. For the examination that Michigan State University developed, a practice book appeared even prior to the first administration of the C2 test (Betsis 2009), based solely on sample tests that appeared on the website (http://www.msu-exams.gr/).

It is interesting to note that there have been numerous criticisms of the testing situation in Greece mainly in terms of the negative impact on English language teaching and student performance. This issue is largely beyond the scope of this paper, but we list some of the salient features, as noted by Tsagari (2009), who conducted an in-depth study on washback effects, that is, the effects of a test on language teaching and learning. She cites three studies (Gabrielatos 1993; Prodromou 1993; Kenny 1995) that have leveled criticism on the effects of the English tests in Greece. The criticisms focused on (1) the overemphasis placed on grammar teaching, (2) teacher-centered lessons, (3) the overemphasis of preparation on test-taking techniques and skills, and (4) a stressful learning environment.

As mentioned above, in order to meet the demands of test takers and the school owners who prepare those students, a large-scale test-preparation publishing industry has emerged which provides practice test books for the various examinations. Another measure of the intensity of these demands is the number of certificates that have been awarded to successful test takers over the years. For example, the University of Cambridge recently reported that the number of Cambridge ESOL certificates issued in Greece has already passed the one-million mark (University of Cambridge 2009).

In sum, the focus in Greece today tends to be more on the examination than on learning language, a point we return to below. Our discussion now turns to our actual experiences in the cross-cultural initiative of test development.

Actual test development

Collaborative underpinnings

The preceding discussion has served as the backdrop to our entry into the Greek context of language teaching and more so language testing. In January of 2007, the President of Anatolia College[1] wrote a letter to the President of Michigan State University (MSU) expressing an interest in partnering with MSU in the development of a test to be administered in Greece. The letter was forwarded to the Director of the English Language Center (Susan Gass) from the President's office. Following lengthy discussions with the Director of the Testing and Certification Division of the English Language Center (Daniel Reed), it was determined that the proposed ideas merited further consideration and so a response was sent to Anatolia College expressing interest.

As a first step, both parties (representatives from Anatolia College and MSU) traveled to Boston for an initial discussion of mutual interests and capabilities. In fact, this turned out to be one of many early meetings as both sides attempted to determine if this partnership would work. At that initial meeting, our goal was to learn as much as possible about the complexities of testing in Greece and what the motivation was for the proposed partnership. Without a doubt this meeting and all subsequent interactions involved learning about the Greek culture. We rapidly learned how difficult it is to get into the mindset of another culture even in a domain that we knew fairly well, that of English language teaching and testing.

From the outset, it was determined that both sides saw the entire enterprise as a collaborative endeavour, if not adventure. In other words, this was a partnership in the true sense of the word, although the purposes of involvement were not always identical. In most instances of large-scale language test development, test developers do not intimately involve the participation of the numerous stakeholders. To the contrary, large-scale testing is typically a top-down endeavor in which testing sets the agenda for curricular and pedagogical decision-making (hence the discussion of 'negative washback'). While there may be focus groups and discussions with experts in language teaching and learning, there is not always a

---

1.   The original letter originally came from the President of Anatolia College and the President of another institution in Greece. Due to a change in administration at the second institution, the project continued only with Anatolia College although the other institution has since joined the team. Anatolia College is a private educational center located in Thessaloniki, Greece. It comprises an elementary school, a secondary school (a preparatory school and an International Baccalaureate program), and a private, non-profit American college that is accredited by NEASC, the New England Association of Schools & Colleges (U.S.A.). Anatolia College and its president agreed to being named in this article.

step-by-step partnership from initial stages of 'why', to actual test development, to test format, to piloting, to test delivery, to test modification, to administration and even to IT logistics. Our approach differed from typical test development activities in that we viewed the entire enterprise as one team with different roles, namely, the U.S. team with the primary responsibility of test development and the Greek team with the responsibility of test administration. As the project moved along, the lines of major responsibility blurred with the Greek team helping with actual test development and the U.S. team helping with administrative aspects of the test. The area of IT involvement was probably the most collaborative and the area most free of cross-cultural difficulties, even though, interestingly, this was the only collaborative area of the project where there were language differences. It was as if the common language of 'computerese' was more important than the natural languages used.

Despite the division of labor, all meetings involved the discussion of all aspects of the test. Further, in the earlier stages of development, the test development team consisted of members from the U.S. and Greece. All parties recognized early on that cultural gaps could rear up at any time. It was therefore determined that the potentiality of culture gaps had to be acknowledged at all phases of the project. We recognized that this was an important part of cross-cultural success, and a system would have to be in place if we were to avoid cultural missteps. To this end, we established a 'culture committee', made up of those living in Greece. Their task was to perform a 'culture' check (or 'cultural sensitivity' check) on items (e.g., reading passages) and essay topics.

In sum, the initiation of the MSU project contrasted with the traditional, unidirectional influence of large-scale testing (negative washback) at least in the sense that there was an explicit attempt to open a serious and extensive dialogue with multiple parties, and to grant each of those parties a significant voice in many crucial aspects of the project. While this collaborative approach did not prevent all of the trademark signs of negative washback (e.g., the appearance of commercial test preparation materials and an emphasis on practice tests in the *frontistiria*), it created the potential for modest reform, the end result of which remains to be seen.

Chronology and content of collaboration

It would be, of course, impossible to chronicle all communication between and among the parties. In this section, we indicate the major points of contact which constituted turning points in the relationship. The most important aspect was to determine first whether we were compatible in terms of personality and working styles (e.g., did everyone have a sense of humor that could get us through successes and failures?). Simply put, we had to first become friends with mutual trust and respect before we could move forward.

The first 'encounter' was the initial letter from the universities in Greece to MSU in which the issues were laid out as was the proposed partnership. This became the entry point into the project. The project was of initial interest to the English Language Center of MSU primarily because it represented an area of academic pursuit different from its everyday activities; it was also felt that it might provide an area of research for Ph.D. students in the Second Language Studies Program at Michigan State University and finally, it could be a general area of graduate student involvement and hence graduate education for both the Ph.D. program and the MA TESOL program. In short, MSU was interested in the proposed project primarily for the purpose of creating new educational opportunities and enhancing existing ones, as opposed to opening up a purely commercial avenue that would generate additional revenue.

Given that we were far from committing ourselves to a project about which we knew little, we engaged in some general correspondence with those who were to be potentially involved. In other words, following the initial letter of invitation from President to President, the project was immediately taken to a level below the level of President. Questions such as "How would this test be different from those already being successfully administered in Greece?" provided us with important information as to what our role might be. We learned at these initial stages what the Greek stakeholders were content with and were not content with with regard to current examinations administered in Greece. In some sense, this provided us with an important insight: the role of school owners, parents, and test-takers in Greece. It also gave us an initial insight into who was not mentioned – those involved in public education, namely, those in the Ministry of Education. Early emails, thus, began to give us a slight vision of who would directly or in most cases indirectly be involved. As noted, interest for the MSU team was sufficiently piqued that the MSU team decided to travel to Boston to meet with representatives of Anatolia College who were to be in Boston for a meeting with their Board of Trustees. In order to give a flavor of the extensive negotiations involved in this problem, below we provide a brief chronology of major meetings and events along with descriptions of content and outcomes.

March 2007

Initial face-to-face meeting. At the first contact meeting, many issues were discussed including the most important one: why another test and why us? We left the meeting feeling confident that we could work to meet their needs, our needs and the interests of all parties. We were also interested in an idea introduced by the Greek team that the project could eventually lead to exchange opportunities for students and teachers, a possibility that was consistent with MSU's educational perspective (as opposed to purely commercial interest) in the collaboration. However, the members of the actual working team from Greece were not present and it was at this level that the feasibility of the working relationship would have to be determined. It was proposed and accepted that the Greek team come to Michigan State University.

April 2007

This was the first face-to-face meeting of the team players. The Greek team consisted of the two lead members involved in the test design, one from each institution, and a second individual from Anatolia College who was responsible for initiatives such as the one being proposed, although he was not involved in language teaching or language testing. It was at this meeting in East Lansing, Michigan that, in addition to determining relationship compatibility, philosophical compatibility in terms of language testing had also to be established. A schedule was worked out for the following visit along with goals for that visit. It was felt that in order to gain an initial understanding of the Greek context, it was important that the MSU team travel to Greece. This was particularly the case since at this meeting in East Lansing it was beginning to become clear to the MSU team that there had to be official recognition by ASEP of the test and that there was a legal process that had to be followed. At this point we were a bit at loose ends not having a clear idea what ASEP was, or what its role was, or what we would have to do to meet the standards established by ASEP.

April/May 2007

Three members of the English Language Center travelled to Greece to meet with team members as well as with the two Presidents of the colleges in Greece. It was the first time that all the members of the teams from each Greek institution met together with MSU representatives to continue discussions about test content, test design, piloting schedule, and steps for official approval.

An important part of these discussions focused on discontent with other tests administered in Greece. A more 'communicative' test was desired, one that utilized authentic language materials and samples of everyday language use (as opposed to one that relied on 'encyclopedic' and scientific or academic content and artificial, language-related tasks). In one historical sense, this request was somewhat ironic in that it echoed some major language testing precedents in Europe. As Spolsky (1995) noted, a significant revision to the University of Cambridge Local Examinations Syndicate (UCLES) examination syllabus in 1974 was based on "...four underlying principles: the communicative approach, the importance of speaking and listening, the authenticity of reading and listening texts, and the 'need to avoid culture bias'. In accepting these, UCLES had shown sensitivity to the major trends in language teaching in general and English language teaching in particular" (Spolsky 1995: 338–339). If the current tests no longer adequately reflected these principles, and if the new MSU examinations were going to constitute a satisfactory improvement (or at least an acceptable alternative), then we knew that our extensive, cross-cultural dialoging had to continue.

July 2007

MSU representatives travelled to Greece and engaged in further (and similar) discussions regarding all aspects of the test. By this time, enough of the test had been developed by the MSU team assembled in East Lansing to begin to think about piloting the test in a Greek context. It was determined that the two tests would not be developed simultaneously; rather, the B2 would be prepared first with the C2 to be ready approximately six months later. What transpired at all of the meetings in Greece was in a sense information gathering; each visit gave us greater insight into a culture that appeared to be quite different from our own. The opportunities for cross-cultural misunderstandings were great despite the fact that all negotiations took place in English with almost all native speakers of English.

November 2007

The first scheduled pilot for the B2 test took place during a September visit to Greece by the MSU team; this was followed up in November by piloting of the revised version of the B2 test. Central to both visits were extensive discussions concerning the approval needed by the independent body known as ASEP. At this point it was becoming clear that this was no easy feat and would involve a number of supporting documents.

April 2008

Nearly one year after the partnership was formed, the first C2 pilot took place. During this visit, extensive classroom observations took place to better understand the type of English language instruction that took place in Greece. This was felt necessary as part of our attempt to generally understand the fuller context of English language testing in Greece. One conclusion from the observations was that students possessed a wide range of abilities. This finding fortunately was compatible with the request for us to develop a test that not only determined who should 'pass' and receive certificates, but also a test that further reported degrees of passing and failing. In addition, it was noted that the classes tended to cover content areas, and then move into important vocabulary and grammar points that were part of the text/theme. In short, the curriculum seemed to be very compatible with our new test design and future goals of increasing the language proficiency of these students (as defined by the CEFR framework).

July 2008

The intent of this meeting in Greece was to make plans for a December administration of the B2 test. It had been understood through verbal communication with ASEP that approval for administration of the MSU test (now known as CELC for the B2 test – Certificate of English Language Competency, and CELP for the C2 test – Certificate of English Language Proficiency) had been granted. However, when the MSU team arrived in Greece, a written communiqué from ASEP made it clear that the approval had to come from the full committee of ASEP which would meet in the Fall. At the summer meeting only a subset of members had been present. We return to a fuller discussion below.

It was during this visit of the MSU team to Greece that issues of promotion and publicity for the test came into the discussion. This raised issues of differing perspectives associated with the different 'cultural' professional backgrounds, that is, marketing versus academia (see section on *another cross-cultural difficulty* below).

Summer 2008

In anticipation of the necessary approvals, a draft of the agreement between Anatolia College and Michigan State University was drawn up. As part of the process, attorneys on both sides reviewed the draft agreement and following numerous email exchanges and revisions, the agreement was signed.

January 2009

Parties from MSU travelled to Greece for a public launch of the new test. This in and of itself was an important new context for the MSU team (see description below).

As noted earlier, the entire process was conceived of as a partnership and development took place with all concerned. That is, even though there were major divisions of labor, both parties were involved with all aspects. Computer programs were developed with IT specialists from both Greece and the U.S. and importantly, formatting and content were frequently discussed and decisions were taken jointly.

Issues of a cross-cultural nature

Intercultural difficulties

We begin this section with an assumption that when dealing cross-culturally, one of the parties always has an incomplete understanding of the other's language (even if highly proficient) and to the relevant knowledge that would be "cued" by the language (Knapp & Knapp-Potthoff 1987). In our context, language was the least of the difficulties. Everyone on the Greek side of the partnership spoke Greek, either natively or following decades of living in Greece. Importantly, all of the active Greek team members were native speakers of American or British English. The U.S. team consisted of native speakers of English with experience living abroad, although not in Greece. All communication within all team meetings was conducted in English, which, as noted, was the native language of the major players. Thus, whatever cross-cultural difficulties occurred were not language dependent.

What turned out to be far more difficult was an understanding of the cultural context in which the test would be administered. Given that there were no serious language difficulties amongst the team members (other than minor British English/American English differences), none of the members realized at the outset how wide the language testing cultural gap was. In other words, we had to first come to the realization that there was a major gulf and then slowly, but surely, understand the components of the gulf and attempt to work to bridge it. This section deals with numerous issues that turned out to be stumbling blocks along the way due to the unfamiliarity of the context; we were without a doubt entering unchartered territory. We were committed to developing a partnership in the true sense of the word, but the partnership was initially formed without fully understanding each other's culture in both a broad and a narrow sense. That is, our Greek partners had to first understand the context that we were working within (e.g., an English Language Center embedded within a U.S. university context) and had to understand the major players at a personal level. Similarly, the U.S. team had to first understand the College context that we were operating within in Greece, the testing context in Greece, the English-language teaching context in Greece, and, of course, the major players at a personal level.

Initial test recognition
One of the first new areas for us was the Greek legal system and particularly the approval needed by ASEP. We mentioned earlier the documentation needed for official recognition, but until we became involved in the process, it was difficult to get the full picture. From the outset we felt like strangers in a strange land. What we understood to be needed was a cover letter by Michigan State University

requesting accreditation by the Greek authority. Accompanying the official letter of request was a letter from the accrediting body of the English Language Center in which our accreditation status (and length of time) is stated. This of course illustrated just one of the cross-cultural difficulties that we encountered since in the U.S. there is no central ministerial approval. University-level accreditation was felt not to be sufficient. Additionally, we had to present the samples of the certificates and a description of the efforts undertaken to ascertain the validity of the test, namely pilot testing in a variety of contexts.

As we moved to gain the necessary approval to have our examination officially accepted as a test of English language ability, our first task was to understand the complexities and necessary maneuverings that would be needed in the months and years to come. For a number of reasons, this proved to be more complex than we had imagined, one being that there were new laws in place for approval to happen and second, seeking clarification was difficult since phones were often not answered and, in general, there was little way to ascertain the status of the process. An extreme example of the latter was the verbal communication mentioned above between the ASEP office and Anatolia College, the entity that was shepherding the MSU application through the process. Many months after all material had been submitted to ASEP, the following email (6/30/2008) was sent from Anatolia College to the Director of the English Language Center at Michigan State University: "President Jackson has spoken on the phone with [a high-level staff member from ASEP] and received confirmation about the positive review of our application. I still do not have anything in writing from them but I expect that they will sooner or later publish this. R. Jackson and [a high-level representative of ASEP] are to speak again over the phone on the 15th of July." On the basis of this positive response, representatives from MSU planned a trip to Greece in July to plan for the first administration of the test in November. When the team arrived in Greece, they met with President Jackson who informed them that he had just received the actual letter from ASEP and, indeed, the discussion at the ASEP meeting had been positive, but the decision had actually been deferred given that the ASEP meeting had not been a full-committee meeting; the waiting game began.

Given the experience of July, we were not certain how to interpret the following email which was received on 10/14/2009: "RJ returned on Friday [..] and this morning he was able to communicate with his office and was told by [a high-level staff member of ASEP] that the issue was discussed and a positive response was given and that we will be notified in writing within the next 'one or two days'". This cultural experience of "yes" and then "no" was something that the MSU representatives were not used to dealing with. We felt we needed to trust our own cultural background 'don't believe it until you have it in writing' and it wasn't until 10/21/2009 with the following email that we were comfortable that this process was behind us: "VICTORY. President Jackson called [...] from Athens and confirmed after reading the document that the process is finally completed". Thus, what was a rollercoaster ride was finally confirmed. Our lack of understanding of how the system worked in another culture led to numerous frustrations and even questioning whether we were on the right path.

Importance of content

Throughout the process of test development, cultural differences were forever paramount. Test items had to address not only the right level of language proficiency, as specified by the CEFR for the examination under development, but also had to be age-appropriate as well as culture-appropriate.[2] Even though this paper will not detail actual issues of test development, it is important to set the context in which we were operating. As mentioned, we were charged with developing two examinations, both situated in relation to CEFR. To do this, we followed the manual titled "Relating language examinations to the Common European Framework of Reference for Languages: Learning, Teaching, Assessment (CEFR)" (2009, http://www.coe.int/T/DG4/Portfolio/documents/Manual%20Revision%20-%20 proofread%20-%20FINAL.pdf, last accessed October 30, 2010). The manual helps in "developing planning tools which provide reference points and common objectives as the basis of a coherent and transparent structure for effective [...] assessment relevant to the needs of learners as well as society, and that can facilitate personal mobility" (2009: 4). This follows on a long tradition beginning with van Ek (1976). In the CEFR manual (2009, reference above), it is stated (p. 4):

> [t]here is no suggestion that different examinations that have been linked to the CEFR by following procedures such as those proposed in this Manual could be considered to be in some way equivalent. Examinations vary in content and style, according to the needs of their context and the traditions of the pedagogic culture in which they are developed [...]. Learners in two different contexts might gain very different scores on (a) an examination whose style and content they are familiar with and (b) an examination at the same level developed for a different context. Secondly, the fact that several examinations may be claimed to be 'at Level B2' as a result of following procedures to link them to the CEFR [...] does not mean that those examinations are claimed to be exactly the same level. B2 represents a band of language proficiency that is quite wide.

This was the academic backdrop against which we began the test development process. In the CEFR Manual, there was discussion of context as well as

---

2. Of course, age and cultural appropriateness are culture-dependent. What level of proficiency can be expected at what age and in what context will differ from culture to culture.

discussion of content and style. Both of these turned out to be important, but not in the way we had originally thought.

An early issue was to ensure that there would not be anything that would be offensive in content. In most instances, this involves common sense. Topics such as religion and politics are to be avoided. However, we were concerned about issues that we might not be aware of that could be interpreted in a way that we could not imagine. We, therefore, set up a cultural sensitive committee made up of those who lived in Greece. We recognized that we did not share the relevant common knowledge (Knapp & Knapp-Potthoff 1987) even though we did share linguistic knowledge. This is different from what Knapp et al. point out is part of intercultural communication where "at least one of the strangers does not speak the language of the interaction as her or his mother tongue" (p. 8). To illustrate this point of sensitivity, we report an incident that happened with another test in Greece in which a writing prompt asked which holiday should be eliminated if one were to eliminate a holiday. Unbeknownst to the test writer, this was a question that had the capacity to offend, given that most holidays in Greece are religious and, of course, it would be offensive to even imagine that a religious holiday could be eliminated. These are 'hidden' intercultural issues that had to be acknowledged and carefully considered and ones that led to the formation of a cultural committee whose responsibility was to vet all content.

As we were developing our writing prompts and speaking prompts, we were constantly mindful of the myriad interpretations that such prompts could have. This often resulted in what was probably an exaggerated censorship. For example, any topic that could ask for candidates' opinion on a controversial topic (e.g., downloading music from the internet) which might be of interest to teenagers, our target audience, might be interpreted by parents as if we were suggesting that an illegal activity could possibly have a positive slant to it.

Responsibility

As mentioned earlier, we entered into our partnership knowing little about the Greek testing and learning context. Our education was trial by fire; each time we travelled to Greece, we came to a better understanding of the role of school owners in the education system. In one of our initial conversations with our partners, it became clear that there were certain perceived weaknesses by school owners that had to be addressed.[3] In minutes from a 04/11/2009 meeting with partners, there was frequent mention of school owners. For example, peppered

---

3. Even though the test was not designed only for students in private schools, it turned out that the most vocal of those with an interest in the tests were the owners of the *frontistiria*, that is, the private schools.

throughout the minutes in which other tests were the topic of discussion were
phrases such as

- *school owners* compared...
- *school owners* remarked...
- ...would not go down favorably with local *school owners* and teachers...
- ...a perennial complaint from *school owner*, teachers and candidates...
- ...another area of concern for *school owners*...
- ...would go down well with *school owners*...
- ...would give *school owners*, teachers, etc. a better opinion of the exam...

(emphases added)

In other words, school owners are important stakeholders who, as consumers of
the test, also figure prominently in decisions made about content, distribution,
and format. As we moved forward with test preparation, our primary concern was
with the academic content of the test, but the need to be mindful of the potential
perceptions of the test was always present. This, of course, is a common concern
of all test developers and particularly those involved in the development of high-
stakes tests.

We were also mindful of the ethical considerations that this conflict brings.
Important in this discussion is the washback on teaching especially given the importance of certificates in the context of our testing. Tsagari (2009) conducted
interviews with students and teachers in her study of the washback effect of the
Cambridge First Certificate. She noted influences in a variety of areas. For example, she notes the following (p. 74):

- emphasis on grammar and vocabulary due to the influence of the exam
- the exam influenced the teaching of writing
- less time on listening due to the weighting of listening
- speaking received little attention
- pronunciation was neglected.

More important than the variable emphasis on skills was Tsagari's comment
(p. 74) about methods: "The majority of the teachers did not employ communicative [tasks] because they thought that these were not compatible with the
principles underlying the exam". The teachers also felt that the Cambridge FCE
influenced their classroom tests. "They believed that the exam influenced their
classroom tests. This influence was mediated through the textbooks they were
using" (p. 74).

Beyond classroom teaching, candidates for the FCE (and all official tests)
engage in intense examination preparation. As can be predicted, the tests are

intimately involved with test preparation. "The examination influenced the types of materials used during the examination preparation period. Teachers used actual past papers and other commercial publications containing model examination questions or supplementary materials focusing on developing language skills needed in the exam" (Tsagari 2009:75). Tsagari (p. 75) goes on to say that "[t]eachers stressed that their methodology was affected by the examination which made them do things they would not otherwise do. In absence of the examination they would employ a communicatively-oriented methodology, focus on individual students' needs, and use more authentic materials". Teachers in general felt that there was pressure on them for their students' success on tests; this included not only the need for school owners to provide specific language instruction, but also for instruction in the general taking of the exam. The dependency on them extended toward parents and employers – this is quite a burden, indeed. Similar feelings were expressed by students: "Students were negative towards communicative activities and any material or activities that did not relate to the exam because they believed that such activities did not relate to the requirements of the exam [...]. They wanted their teachers to provide them with 'repeated items' and they would get upset if their teachers were not able to prepare them adequately for what was to come in the exam" (p. 76).

The preceding was intended to give a picture of the context of test development. Despite the discussions of this testing culture, it was difficult to imagine how pervasive it was until we experienced it directly. In January 2009, we participated in a launch of the new MSU-Anatolia test. This in and of itself was a new cultural experience, especially because it became a media event with photographers and reporters. The beginning part of the event involved a presentation of the background to the development of the new test, followed by information pertaining to the test itself, namely, the format and a description of the content. After the presentation part, there were questions from the floor. One question was particularly noteworthy. This came from a school owner who was somewhat angry that she would have only three months to prepare her students for this exam. As applied linguists with a reasonable understanding of how language learning and language teaching work, we were somewhat surprised that teaching English at a level appropriate for the examination would not be considered sufficient. B2 knowledge should be the same for any test purporting to assess that construct. Nonetheless, the comment was an eye-opener into another culture and, in particular, helped us get into the mindset of how school owners think. It was truly an example of how one could be 'talked at' about a context, but had to 'live it' to be able to truly understand it.

Perhaps none of this should have been surprising, as our experience with language and cultural issues parallels well-documented concerns in language testing. The importance of (and the distinction between) language and socio-cultural competence features prominently in the literature on the development of the CEFR. In fact, the notion "sociolinguistic knowledge" is discussed extensively in the CEFR main text (Council of Europe 2001). Unfortunately, these concerns have not been well resolved. North (2000) concludes that "Socio-cultural competence appears to remain an area which needs to be scaled, if it can be scaled, entirely separately from language proficiency" (North 2000: 348).

Another cross-cultural difficulty

There is another important cross-cultural difficulty that we encountered although this had nothing to do with language or with national cultural differences. This had to do with conducting an academic project in a competitive business context. In particular, we were academics engaged in an academic enterprise; we were not prepared to participate in a 'campaign' to promote our test. One example of this occurred when the advertising team in Greece came up with a clever ad campaign which seemed less than professional to us in consideration of the academic context in which we operated. This resulted in some bad feelings because the Greek advertising team felt that the campaign they had envisioned was clever enough to win an advertising award in Greece. The U.S. team felt that it was not the type of campaign that would fit in well with the academic mission of our university. This was a cultural rift that had to be delicately balanced so that the relationship could stay on a positive footing.

Understanding the Greek certificate culture

In one of our early meetings, we were informed of the Greek certificate culture. In fact, even prior to face-to-face meetings, the initial letter to the President of Michigan State University made note of this: "The Greek market has a unique 'certificate' culture...". In other words, students were used to taking numerous examinations for the purpose of getting certificates. This topic came up again and again and is also referred to in Tsagari's (2009) book. Hardly a meeting went by without this being mentioned.

Because certificates have such an important role in Greek society, all aspects of the test and the certificate itself assume importance. For example, formatting and the entire physical appearance of the test were deemed important. The paper that the actual certificates are printed on was also important. And, finally, grading the writing part of the test had to take place in the U.S. for the test to have credibility.

Stakeholders

Following the second administration of the test, Anatolia College distributed a questionnaire to students and school owners asking questions about the ease of the registration process, the adequacy of prior information of the test and, important for our purposes, questions that related to the role of English and testing in Greece. The statements for students are given below:

- living in Greece, it is important to know English
- the changing role of English includes an increasing need for 'communicative' abilities with the language rather than just knowledge of grammar and vocabulary
- it is important to take courses that specifically prepare me for each test that I will take (e.g., MSU-CELC, ECCE [the test produced by the University of Michigan], FCE [the test of Cambridge University]).

Responses were on a four point scale ranging from Strongly Agree to Strongly Disagree. With the exception of one student who responded "Disagree" to the first question, all responses (14 students) were either Strongly Agree/Agree to all questions. In other words, they recognized the need to have communicative abilities. Yet, they also felt a need for separate preparation for each examination.

Students were also asked to rank in order of importance four statements regarding the importance of having certificates of English language competency and/or proficiency:

- my friends have certificates
- my parents want me to have certificates
- I can get a better job with a certificate
- my future depends on my having a certificate.

The results are given in Table 1.

The responses to these questions were relatively uniform. All students ranked the first two at the bottom of the list and the questions relating to jobs and future at the top. Thus, the notion of peer and parental pressure appears to have taken a back seat to more utilitarian goals.

A similar questionnaire was sent to school owners (*frontistiria*). Six responses were received. As was the case with the student questionnaire, school owners were asked to order in terms of importance the following four statements:

- my school will be considered more prestigious if my students obtain certificates
- parents will be pleased if their children obtain certificates

Table 1. Responses from students (n = 14)

Responses	# stating this as most important	# stating this as 2nd most important	# stating this as 3rd most important	# stating this as least important
My friends have certificates.			6	7*
My parents want me to have certificates.			7	6*
I can get a better job with a certificate.	10.5**	3.5		
My future depends on my having a certificate.	3.5**	10.5		

* One person did not respond to this question.
** Half numbers are used when an individual checked two boxes, but did not rank the answers; half point was given to each.

Table 2. Responses from school owners (n = 6)

Responses	# stating this as most important	# stating this as 2nd most important	# stating this as 3rd most important	# stating this as least important
My school will be considered more prestigious if my students obtain certificates.	1.5*	3		1
Parents will be pleased if their children obtain certificates.	2.5	1	2	
My students will be better quali-fied to enter the work-force if they have certificates.	2		2	1.5
My students will enjoy a better future if they have certificates.		1	1	3.5

* Half numbers are used when an individual checked two boxes, but did not rank the answers or ranked responses equally; half point was given to each.

– my students will be better qualified to enter the work-force if they have certificates
– my students will enjoy a better future if they have certificates.

The results were not as uniform as the students' response, but they do indicate a trend. The results can be seen in Table 2.

What was surprising was that the issues of prestige and pleasing parents were strong motivators for school owners. Further, we had not anticipated that school owners did not see the certificates as particularly important with regard to the work force or a better future, in stark contrast with student responses. The small sample of respondents may not, however, be representative.

Conclusion

In conclusion, in developing tests, and we would argue, even in developing peda-gogical materials, it is crucial that all involved have a complete understanding of the cultural context. Given the inevitable gaps in cultural knowledge by all parties at the outset, a sincerely collaborative approach was the only reasonable course to take. It is a delicate task to balance sociocultural and even political demands on the one hand with the needs to be rigorous and ethical in test development on the other. In our instance, we were aided by a cooperative team concept that allowed us to work through cultural differences on both sides. Most important is the fact that there needs to be a sensitivity to intercultural issues if there is to be a successful outcome. These considerations also apply in any discussion of the responsibilities and limitations of language testers (cf. Fulcher & Davidson 2007; Hamp-Lyons 2001; Davies 1997; Shohamy 2000, 2001). In particular, our approach seems to be consistent with Shohamy's plea to involve all stakehold-ers in major decision-making activities (Shohamy 2001: 147–148). Finally, even though intercultural difficulty usually involves language difficulties, our case of test development in an environment new to the developers showed the difficul-ties to be not about language at all. It was about attitudes, goals, and context; it was about moving between testing in the U.S. and testing in Greece; and it was about moving between an academic context and a business context. A full under-standing of all of these factors and pressures is necessary for smooth travels from beginning to end.

References

Betsis, A. 2009. *Succeed in Michigan State University CELP, Level C2.* Athens: Andrew Betsis ELT.

Council of Europe. 2001. *A Common European Framework of Reference for Languages: Learn-ing, teaching, assessment.* Cambridge: CUP.

Davies, A. 1997. Introduction: The limits of ethics in language testing. *Language Testing* 14: 235–241.

Fulcher, G. & Davidson, F. 2007. *Language Testing and Assessment: An Advanced Resource book.* London: Routledge.

Gabrielatos, C. 1993. Learning how to fish: Fostering fluency and independence. *TESOL Greece Newsletter* 38: 23–26.

Hamp-Lyons, L. 2001. Ethics, fairness(es) and developments in language testing. In *Experimenting with Uncertainty: Essays in honour of Alan Davies. Studies in Language Testing* 11, C. Elder, A. Brown, E. Grove, K. Hill, N. Iwashita, T. Lumley, T. McNamara & K. O'Loughlin (eds), 222–227. Cambridge: CUP.

Kenny, N. 1995. The new FCE reading paper. *ELT NEWS* 74: 15.

Knapp, K. & Meierkord, C. (eds). 2002. *Lingua Franca Communication*. Frankfurt: Peter Lang.

Knapp, K. & Knapp-Potthoff, A. 1987. Instead of an introduction: Conceptual issues in analyzing intercultural communication. In *Analyzing Intercultural Communication*, K. Knapp, W. Enninger & A. Knapp-Potthoff (eds), 1–13. Berlin: Mouton de Gruyter.

Meierkord, C. &. Knapp, K. 2002. Approaching lingua franca communication. In *Lingua Franca Communication*, K. Knapp & C. Meierkord (eds), 9–28. Frankfurt: Peter Lang.

North, B. 2000. *The Development of a Common European Framework*. Bern: Peter Lang.

Phillipson, R. 2003. *English-only Europe?: Challenging Language Policy*. London: Routledge.

Prodromou, L. 1993. The great Greek paperchase: Still waiting for the examiners – A national sport. *Foreign Language Education Review* 52: 9–10.

Seidlhofer, B., Breiteneder, A. & Pitzl, M. L. 2006. English as a lingua franca in Europe. *Annual Review of Applied Linguistics* 26: 3–34. Cambridge: CUP.

Shohamy, E. 2000. Fairness in language testing. In *Fairness and Validation in Language Assessment* [Studies in Language Testing 9], A. J. Kunnan (ed.), 15–19. Cambridge: CUP.

Shohamy, E. 2001. *The Power of Tests: A Critical Perspective on the Uses of Language Tests*. London: Longman.

Spolsky, B. 1995. *Measured Words*. Oxford: OUP.

Tsagari, D. 2009. *The Complexity of Test Washback*. Frankfurt: Peter Lang.

University of Cambridge, Press Release. 2009. Cambridge Brings 800 Years of Experience to Greece. (February 5, 2009). <http://www.cambridgeesol.org/assets/pdf/what-we-do/newsroom/press_800_years_greece050209.pdf> (Febr. 27, 2010).

van Ek, J. A. 1976. *The Threshold Level for Modern Language Learning in Schools*. Strasbourg: Council of Europe.

When comprehension is crucial

Using English as a medium of instruction at a German university

Annelie Knapp
University of Siegen, Germany

After a brief discussion of the increasing importance of English in the lives of German university students, this article focuses on how the use of English as a non-native language in university lectures and seminars may affect the structure of these communicative events and their potential for the acquisition of knowledge. An analysis of empirical data from courses in Economics, Political Sciences and Chemistry (questionnaires and discourse data) provides some insights into students' perceptions of the problems and benefits of English-medium instruction as well as into the strategies that students and lecturers use to support comprehension and to negotiate meaning while using English as a lingua franca for teaching and learning at a German university.

1.   Introduction: English in the lives of German university students

As in many other areas of life, the use of the English language is gaining ground in German Higher Education. The spread of English into German universities has affected practically all subjects and all levels of university education. With the continued introduction of English-taught programmes since the 1990s and, in addition, an increasing number of individual courses taught in English, students and lecturers alike do not only have to cope with a rapidly growing body of academic texts written in English, but also with oral communication in English as their non-native language during lectures, seminars and exams.

For reasons that will be discussed below, many universities show a pronounced interest in promoting the use of English in university studies. Some universities, e.g. the University of Erfurt, even urge their lecturers to offer English-medium instruction. In April 2009, the vice-president for international affairs at the University of Erfurt appealed to all lecturers at the University of Erfurt to offer more teaching in English. At least two courses per faculty and semester have to be held in English now, and the description of courses in the university calendar in German and in English has been made compulsory.

The various factors responsible for the general spread of English are well-known: Coleman (2006:2), making reference to Clyne (1984), mentions "economic, political and strategic alliances", "scientific, technological and cultural cooperation", "mass media", "multinational corporations", "improved communications" and – more generally – "the internationalization of professional and personal domains of activity". Yet, a set of specific factors as rationales for the introduction of English-medium instruction in Higher Education has to be considered as well (Coleman 2006:4ff.). These factors are interrelated and support each other. Growing student mobility is just one of them. A considerable number of German students spend a term or more studying abroad. In 2009, 26% of German students reported a study-related stay abroad, 50% of them had studied at a foreign university (DAAD 2009[1]). In return, more than 233,000 students from abroad studied at German universities (DAAD 2009,[2] data from 2008). In 2008, 9.2% of all students at German universities were foreign students (incoming students from abroad[3]), and Germany holds 10% of the international student market share (Varghese 2008:18; data from 2004), only outnumbered by the US and the UK (for more detailed information see Wächter & Maiworm 2008). International student mobility is desirable for political as well as for economic reasons: Germany is trying to get its share of the international education market, and without English-taught programmes there would be hardly a chance in the competition for foreign students. Partly as a consequence, partly as a precondition for internationalisation, teaching materials written in English are used with increasing frequency, thus contributing to English-based teaching.

Another push factor for offering courses in English at German universities relates to students' future prospects on the labour market. Proficiency in the English language and, in particular, a high degree of proficiency in English for professional communication is regarded as beneficial for graduate employability. In order to achieve this goal, supplying additional tuition in English as a foreign language is no longer regarded as the optimal – or even the only – solution. Rather, the

---

1.   See <http://www.wissenschaft-weltoffen.de/daten/4/4>. The data are based on: HIS-Studie: Internationale Mobilität der deutschen Studierenden. Studienbezogene Aufenthalte in anderen Ländern.

2.   See <http://www.wissenschaft-weltoffen.de/daten/1/1/2>. The data are based on: Studentenstatistik Statistisches Bundesamt and calculations by HIS.

3.   See <http://www.wissenschaft-weltoffen.de/daten/1/1/3>. The data are based on: Studentenstatistik Statistisches Bundesamt and calculations by HIS.

integration of content and language learning is seen to have many advantages: the acquisition of subject specific terminology in English as well as the acquisition of subject or domain specific linguistic means of communicating about subject matter, including the realisation of typical academic language functions in English. In addition, practical and economical reasons play a role for integrating content and language learning in university studies. The mismatch between the increasing demands on students in terms of knowledge and competences to be acquired and – at the same time – a shorter time span for university studies contribute to the attractiveness of a 'getting two for the price of one' solution. This kind of reasoning fits nicely into the broader educational context. In Germany, as in other parts of Europe, the concept of Content and Language Integrated Learning (CLIL) is generally regarded as a most promising concept for teaching foreign languages at school. CLIL is considered to have positive effects on language learning as well as on content learning, and it is seen as a useful preparation for meeting future job-related linguistic demands (see, for example, Marsh & Wolff 2007; Vollmer 2005; Wolff 2009). The claims about positive effects of CLIL need to be substantiated, however, by more empirical evidence.

Last, but not least, a special field of Higher Education has to be considered: the field of teacher training. The increasing requirements with regard to the level of foreign language ability in many areas of life have also had an impact on the demands made on the linguistic competence of teachers of English. Different from what used to be normal a couple of decades ago, instruction for future teachers of English now takes place predominantly in English.

The spread of English in German university studies, convincing, necessary and inevitable as it may seem, has, however, been observed with some concern and has even met with criticism of a very fundamental nature (see, for example, Ammon 1998, 2006; Carli & Ammon 2007; Ammon & McConnell 2002; Ehlich 2000, 2005; Graddol 1997). Relevant arguments refer to fears of linguistic dominance or even imperialism, the danger of a substantial reduction of linguistic diversity and a concomitant loss of language-specific conceptualisations and nuances of meaning. On a more concrete level, problems of putting non-native speakers of English at a disadvantage in terms of time and effort needed as well as in terms of communicative success have to be taken seriously.

German students themselves show some ambivalence with regard to English-medium instruction (EMI). As will be shown in more detail below (Section 3), some students seem to appreciate the chance to improve their English language abilities during university courses and to develop their academic English in particular. On the other hand, some of them are worried about the effect that problems of comprehension and of expressing themselves adequately in test situations may have on their marks. They are aware of the fact that in university

teaching comprehension is a crucial aspect of their academic success and therefore show a certain reluctance to participate in EMI.

The main focus of this article will not be on the political and economic issues,
but rather on the practice of English-medium instruction in a university context,
on students' perceptions of its benefits and challenges, on teaching strategies and
opportunities for learning and – last but not least – on patterns of communication in contexts of English-medium teaching. This focus, involving a shift to the
micro-level of English-medium instruction, makes it necessary to introduce a few
distinctions, because "English-medium instruction" is a cover term for a range of
communicative situations which, although having a lot in common, also differ
from each other in relevant ways.

2.   Instructional discourse as lingua franca discourse and as EMI discourse

In spite of the growing numbers of EMI courses at German universities (and elsewhere in Europe as well) the implications for teaching and learning in an L2 are
anything but clear. The idea of 'getting two for the price of one' is certainly too
simplistic and too optimistic. Specific questions on what kinds of advantages and
what kinds of problems can be expected have to be asked – and answered. Two
contradicting hypotheses should be considered here: (1) EMI at universities is
beneficial for both language learning and subject matter learning (or – a weaker
version: it does not affect subject matter learning in a negative way) and (2) EMI
leads to less satisfactory results than instruction in the students' L1, mainly because there may be severe problems of comprehension. Of course, both hypotheses should be specified with regard to the conditions under which EMI takes
place, e.g. the level of lecturers' and students' competence in English. It seems
reasonable to assume that the positive effects of EMI can only unfold beyond a
certain threshold level.

In order to achieve the necessary differentiation, the concepts and terminology
that will be used in the following discussion have to be defined more precisely.

The term *instructional discourse* will be used to refer to any interaction in an
institutionalised context whose aim is the increase of knowledge and skills of the
majority of the participants. Characteristically, there is at least one person who
is more knowledgeable in the area that is the object of instruction. The adjective *instructional* must not be taken too literally, however: it does not necessarily
imply the transmission of knowledge, but may also refer to more modern conceptualisations of teaching–learning arrangements, where the 'instructor' creates

favourable conditions for the acquisition of knowledge and the development of competencies in a variety of ways.

The term *lingua franca discourse* will be (and has so far been) used as commonly defined: lingua franca discourse takes place when two or more persons who do not share an L1 make use of another language in which both (or all) communicators are competent to a certain degree for communicative purposes (see, e.g. Knapp & Meierkord 2002; Mauranen & Ranta 2009). If native speakers of the language that is chosen as a lingua franca take part in the discourse, it will still be considered as lingua franca discourse. Note that in this article no claims are being made about whether English as a lingua franca (ELF) should be considered as a variety of English or not, and no claims are made about a special status for ELF-medium instruction or ELF-medium instructional discourse.

English-medium instruction (EMI) is a term that is used for any institutionalised teaching-learning situation in which communication takes place in English, although the majority of participants are non-native speakers of English. Thus, the term *EMI* may refer to teaching-learning situations where English is being used as a lingua franca as well as to teaching-learning situations where participants share the same L1, but where nevertheless English is used.

The diversity of reasons for enhancing English-medium instruction, as briefly described above, has led to different set-ups for the use of English in university teaching. At least three types should be distinguished:

Type 1: EMI in international programmes.

Type 2: EMI for students of English linguistics and literature and future teachers of English.

Type 3: EMI for German students of any subject, with the goal of preparing them for studying abroad and/or the use of English in their future professional lives.

This distinction is necessary for taking adequate and differentiated account of what is happening in EMI classrooms.

Type 1 definitely leads to a lingua franca situation. Making use of the English language is absolutely necessary to achieve understanding, as there is no alternative of falling back on somebody's L1. The lingua franca situations may be extremely complex in this type of set-up. In a course in engineering from which we collected data in the context of our research project "Mehrsprachigkeit und Multikulturalität im Studium" ("Multilingualism and multiculturalism in university studies") there were 23 students from 13 countries with 14 different L1s; only one of them – apart from the lecturer – was German. For each of the participants this meant that he/she had to be able to comprehend various native as well as learner varieties of English. The goals to be reached in this type of set-up refer predominantly or even exclusively to an increase in subject matter knowledge. The English language is just a vehicle for teaching and learning subject matter.

In type 2 there is much more homogeneity with regard to participants' L1. In these courses, particularly so if they are courses for future language teachers, there is hardly ever a person who does not have German as (one of) his/her first language(s). The lecturer may, however, be a native speaker of English, usually with a good command of German as an L2. Thus, if necessary, participants can draw on their common knowledge of another language than English. Moreover, there is much more homogeneity in cultural terms than in type 1 – a factor that may affect communication and therefore comprehension in decisive ways. In type 2 courses the improvement of competence in the English language is an additional goal – with a focus not only on communicative success, but also on grammatical correctness and native-like pronunciation.

In type 3 set-ups there is no necessity to use the English language. The underlying rationale is rather that being able to communicate about subject matter in English would be an additional asset for the students – to prepare them for studying abroad and/or for their future professional lives. The majority of students in this set-up have German as their L1, and the occasional students with an L1 other than German usually have a decent command of German as well. Therefore, relying on German as a common language is also an option here. In contrast to set-up 2, growth in language competence is intended, but not essential. Communicative success is generally more important than grammatical correctness.

University lectures and seminars are particular genres of discourse, which place specific demands on participants. Therefore, EMI at universities must be treated as an object of research in its own right, since it differs in characteristic ways from other types of discourse which involve the use of a foreign language. First of all, as stated above, EMI discourse is not necessarily lingua franca discourse. If it is, it is so to a certain degree, showing a lot of variation in terms of how many native speakers of English take part, how many participants share a common L1 and how many different L1s are involved. The number of participants in an EMI situation varies. It may be more than a hundred, but it may also be as small as three. Normally, there is a lecturer who controls the discourse and who allocates turns of speaking, thus imposing restrictions on spontaneous negotiations of meaning, which seem to be characteristic of other types of lingua franca discourse. With larger numbers of participants, EMI discourse tends towards a lecture with a basically monological character and only few dialogical sub-sequences. With smaller numbers of participants, there is a tendency towards more interaction, but EMI discourse is hardly ever a dialogue between just two people. During dialogic sequences within EMI discourse the other participants, as bystanders, are indirectly involved as well and may benefit from (or be irritated by) dialogues between other speakers.

Furthermore it has to be taken into account that EMI discourse is institutional discourse. Participants are bound to a certain spatial and temporal framework, and deviating from this framework is hardly possible.

It is a common characteristic of all types of instructional discourse that they have clearly defined goals. As instructional discourse, they aim at an increase in knowledge, competencies and/or skills, i.e. at learning, with (usually) one person, the lecturer, standing out from the others in being the more knowledgeable one and in being mainly responsible for the intended increase in knowledge and competencies of the other participants in the discourse. This makes it necessary for the participants to comprehend as much as possible of what is being said, to process and store the acquired knowledge and, in addition, to be able to reproduce or use and apply it later on. Of course, this description is a gross simplification of the complex mental processes involved, but in our context it may be sufficient for raising awareness of the fact that comprehension is crucial in instructional discourse. Different from other types of ELF discourse that have been investigated, the strategy of "letting it pass" (Firth 1996) does not seem wise and may be even counter-productive in instructional discourse. In Section 4, we will discuss an example in which the lecturer even explicitly encourages students to refrain from "letting it pass".

Because of the extraordinary relevance of comprehension in instructional discourse, oral interaction is often supplemented and supported by written material: handouts, scripts, textbooks, Powerpoint presentations and notes on the board.

Another characteristic of instructional discourse refers to discrepancies with regard to the participants' knowledge base: overcoming differences in knowledge is the very goal of instructional discourse. This fact is likely to have implications for communication in EMI contexts, since there is usually less common ground that can be taken for granted than in other types of discourse and therefore less potential for the successful construction of meaning. It seems reasonable to assume that comprehension gets more difficult when a lack of shared subject knowledge, which is characteristic of instructional discourse, is combined with a lack of shared linguistic resources and cultural background knowledge.

EMI at universities may well be regarded as a type of Content and Language Integrated Learning (CLIL). One has to be careful, however, not to draw premature parallels between EMI at universities and CLIL in the school context, since, again, conditions and circumstances differ. Just a few factors will be mentioned here. CLIL at school is much more homogeneous than EMI at universities, in terms of variety of L1 background as well as in terms of size of the groups.

Furthermore, relatively fixed groups of learners and teachers interact more regularly and over longer periods of time than at university. They have, as a consequence, more opportunities to get used to each other's accents and communicative styles and to establish common conventions of communicating. In addition, CLIL as practised in the school context is normally supplemented by 'ordinary' English language teaching, and normally EFL teachers and CLIL teachers cooperate with each other – if they are not the same person anyhow. Many CLIL teachers at school are competent in both subject matter teaching and foreign language teaching and can find various types of support, as far as specific CLIL materials or CLIL-specific didactic approaches are concerned. None of these is the case with university lecturers teaching their subject in English. Respective training programmes for university lecturers are just beginning to be developed.

In the following sections, we will take a closer look at practices of communicating, teaching and learning in English at a German university. We will present findings from a series of empirical studies of EMI, starting with some results of a questionnaire study which investigates German students' attitudes towards EMI and which was carried out in a type 3 set-up (see above). We will continue with a discussion of data from a course in Applied Chemistry, where English is used as a lingua franca (type 1 set-up; see above).

3.   Getting nothing for the price of two? German students' perceptions of (and attitudes towards) English-medium instruction

In a questionnaire study with 96 bachelor students from the University of Siegen, we tried to explore students' perceptions of EMI. In two English-taught courses in Economics (22 participants) and Political Sciences (18 participants), we asked students about comprehension problems, about their participation in class, about how well they felt prepared for EMI, and what kinds of benefits and disadvantages they saw in EMI. These data were supplemented by data from a German-taught course in Economics on the same topic (56 participants), which the students could attend in the following semester as an alternative to the course held in English. The questionnaire consisted of a combination of closed format and open format questions. Just a selection of the most interesting results will be presented here. For a more detailed and comprehensive presentation of results see Knapp and Münch (2008).

Avoidance

The data from the course in Economics that was taught in German show a notable tendency for students to avoid courses taught in English. Four students (out of 46) stated that they had started with the EMI course, but abandoned it in favour of the course taught in German. Another 11 students (out of the 25 students who were aware of the same course being offered in English) had deliberately chosen the course taught in German in the first place.The main reasons given for not choosing the EMI course were: concerns about bad marks, the additional time needed for learning subject matter in English, and insufficient knowledge of English.

Problems of comprehension

64% of the students attending the EMI courses in Economics and Political Science stated that they experienced occasional problems of comprehension. Another 8% stated that they experienced comprehension problems frequently. More than half of the students (56%) classified their problems as language-related, compared to 32% who regarded their problems as content-related. About 12% regarded their comprehension problems as related to both language and content. There was no significant difference between the courses in Economics and in Political Sciences (see Hellekjaer 2004 for comparable findings in Norway; see also Snow Andrade 2006 for a review of research on the adjustment and academic achievement of international students in English-speaking universities).

Preparedness for EMI

61% of the students in the two EMI courses with German as their L1 felt that school had prepared them well (50%) or even very well (11%) for EMI. 22% regarded their preparation as sufficient and 17% as bad or non-existent. The data from the Economics course that was taught in German showed a remarkable difference in the students' self-assessment of their English instruction at school: apart from the almost identical proportion of students who felt very well prepared (11%), only 28% compared to 50% in the EMI courses felt well prepared for EMI. Another 48% regarded their preparation as sufficient. Two possibilities suggest themselves to explain this discrepancy: either more students from the German-taught course had experienced difficulties with EMI (and therefore preferred the course taught in German), or they were not confident enough to attend an EMI course, anticipating difficulties with EMI without actually having experienced them. In any case, it is obvious that avoidance of EMI does not allow students to benefit from EMI. Furthermore, the fact that only half of the students from the three courses felt well or very well prepared for EMI is a cause for concern and calls for measures to bridge the gap between the competencies in the English language acquired at school and the demands of university studies in English.

Further problems of EMI

In answers to an open question about further problems, the students attending EMI courses mentioned additional problems as being specific to EMI, apart from problems of comprehension. Arranged according to frequency, these problems were: less participation on the part of the students, lack of subject-specific vocabulary, higher demands, problems of motivation, less discussion, reduction of contents, and need for reviewing the contents. Only two of the students did not see any problems at all.

The students from the course taught in German were asked to answer an open question about what kinds of problems they would expect in English-taught courses. Besides problems of comprehensibility and lack of subject-specific vocabulary – the two most frequent responses – the following problems and difficulties were mentioned: difficulties in test situations, a negative impact on marks, a lot of time and effort needed, negative effects on content learning, increased difficulty of the course, less oral participation.

Benefits of EMI

The students' concerns about negative effects of EMI are, however, outweighed by a much larger number of reasons given in favour of attending EMI courses: almost two thirds of the German students participating in the two EMI courses expect a positive effect on their language abilities in English, about 30% expect positive learning effects in general, and about 10% regard EMI as useful for their future jobs. The students from the course taught in German, too, show a pronounced awareness of the benefits of EMI. Altogether, they mention 53 arguments in favour of EMI, compared to 18 arguments against it. The majority of arguments (26) refer to the improvement of their language abilities, followed by usefulness for their future jobs.

In summary, the results of this small-scale study suggest that students are well aware of the advantages of EMI, but that they are nevertheless concerned about a potentially negative impact on their academic success and about the additional workload resulting from the use of a foreign language for instruction. A preliminary conclusion to be drawn is that students' additional effort in struggling with EMI should be appreciated in some way rather than result in bad marks. Furthermore, students should be supported in acquiring the linguistic competencies and skills that are necessary for participating in EMI.

4.   Don't let it pass! Achieving comprehension in *lingua franca* instructional discourse: An example from a course in chemistry

The following discussion is based on data recorded in four sessions of a course in Applied Chemistry in the context of an International Master Programme. The lecturer is a native speaker of German, the students (between 8 and 10 in number) have a variety of L1 backgrounds and differ considerably in their proficiency in English. One of the students is American with English as her first language and a good command of German. So this is clearly a lingua franca situation.

Our first example shows the lecturer using a strategy that may also be part of his strategic repertoire for lectures and seminars in L1 contexts: in trying to explain the meaning of the term *chelate cycle* the lecturer draws on linguistic and cultural knowledge which he seems to take for granted as shared knowledge on the part of (at least some of) the course participants. This strategy turns out, however, to be based on assumptions that are not completely adequate.

Example (1): Chelate cycle[4]

L: lecturer; S: student; Ss: several students:
The students numbered S1, S2 etc. may be different students in each of the examples.

L:	does anybody know chelate cycle? (--) chelate cycle (..) who knows what that is? (---)
L:	doesn't anybody speak Greek or Latin?
Several Ss:	(*laughter*) no (..) no
L:	still nobody
Several Ss:	(*trying to repeat the word*) Kilots? Kilos?

---

4. For reasons of readability, comprehensibility and ease of processing, the transcripts are presented in conventional writing. Only the following specific transcription conventions are used:

(.)	micro-pause
(-)	pause of approximately 0.25–1 second ((-) or (--) or (---) according to its duration)
(2.0)	estimated length of pause (more than 1 second)
ACcent	primary or main accent

L:	(*to the only student with English as L1*) what is Krebs?
S1 (USA)	crabs
L:	crabs?
S1 (USA):	crab or a lobster
L:	you know this animal with eight legs (-) which animal has also eight legs?
Several Ss:	spider
S2 (Macedonia):	aaah (..) *chelots!*
L:	yes, which language is this?
S2 (Macedonia):	this language is Macedonian (..) we are on a border with Greece.
L:	I use the English pronunciation of chelates (/'ki:leɪts/.) (*writes word on the board*)
S3 (China):	tschelos?
All Ss and L:	(*laughter*)
L:	we don't care about pronunciation. (*describes the similarity between the chemical procedure and a crab, trying to grasp food with its claw*) it has a claw finger (-) there are elements (-) the claw picks one element (..) it is selective (..) this is the chelate cycle (..) Chelat-Ring auf Deutsch (---) this here is phenanthroline. (*describes phenanthroline and chelate cycle, making use of an illustration in a script that is also projected on the wall*)
Several Ss:	(*nodding; one of the students makes grasping-movements with his hands*) mmhmm (..) mmhmm[5]

This digression to negotiate meaning lasted for almost two minutes. Was it worth it? On the one hand, one might argue that it was a waste of time to discuss the term so intensively. On the other hand, one could argue that precisely this negotiation process may have contributed significantly to the depth of processing and, as a consequence, retention of this term and comprehension of the respective concept.

What is noticeable in this example as well is the strong focus on meaning. The lecturer sees pronunciation as less important.

---

5. "The word chelation is derived from Greek χηλή, *chelè*, meaning claw; the ligands lie around the central atom like the claws of a lobster." (Wikipedia: Chelation)

"The term *chelate* was first applied in 1920 by Sir Gilbert T. Morgan and H. D. K. Drew, who stated: "The adjective chelate, derived from the great claw or *chele* (Greek) of the lobster or other crustaceans, is suggested for the caliperlike groups which function as two associating units and fasten to the central atom so as to produce heterocyclic rings."

Morgan, Gilbert T.; Drew, Harry D. K. (1920). "CLXII – Researches on residual affinity and co-ordination. Part II. Acetylacetones of selenium and tellurium". *J. Chem. Soc., Trans.* 117: 1456. (Wikipedia: Chelation)

Let us look at some more examples from another session of the same course.

Example (2): Shovels, arrays and ditches

In introducing the topic of sampling techniques, the lecturer starts with asking the students what kind of sampling techniques they have already heard of. One of the students answers that he has heard about coal-quartering. The lecturer's question if everybody knows what it means, is answered unisono with "No". The lecturer explains the procedure:

L:	ok (..) you take a bucket, collect a sample.

(*more explanations follow*)

L:	you take a shovel. (--) do you say shovel?
S1 (US):	yes
Ss:	yes, yes, shovel

(*more explanations follow*)

L:	we put a Schablone (..) what is Schablone auf Englisch?
S1 (US):	I don't know
L:	who knows Schablone in English?
Ss	no(..) no don't know
S1 (US):	ah, an array

Later on:

L:	ditches (-) do you say that? (-) oh my English is so bad (..) I don't know (-) Gräben (..) it has ups and downs, valleys, high points
S1 (US):	oh troughs?

This example shows that the lecturer has some problems in finding the correct English words for expressing the intended meaning. He is supported by the native speaker of English, which leads to a joint construction of utterances.

Example (3): Sesame Street

Later on in this session, the lecturer talks about smoke stack sampling. The specific topic is PAH (polycyclic aromatic hydrocarbons).

L:	do you know PAHs?

(*pause, no one volunteers to answer*)

L:	do you know Sesame Street?
S1 (US):	yes
L:	you must know (..) what about others? (...) do you know Sesame Street?

(*no verbal reaction; some students shake their heads*)

L:	you don't watch TV?
S2:	(*unintelligible*)

L: you don't have transmissions for children in your home?
(*pause – no one replies*)
L: they train watchers to ask questions (...) you have to ask questions or you
            will die stupid (--) so if i mention you something and you don't know?
(*pause, no reaction*)
L: carefully listen and sleep?
Ss: (*laughter*)
L: it is your duty to ask
S3:   or you will continue
Ss: (*laughter*)
L: you are here to learn (--) there are no stupid questions (..) just stupid
            answers (-)... so what are PAHs?
(*lecturer explains the abbreviation, draws a picture on the board, students now answer
questions, repeat words*)

This example shows how the lecturer tries to encourage his students to be more
active in using strategies for achieving comprehension. "Ask questions if you don't
understand" is the message he wants to get across. Or, to express it in linguistic
terms: make use of clarification requests to enhance comprehension. However,
the lecturer initiates this sequence in a rather peculiar way. In an attempt to relate
what is going on in the course to everyday life, he makes reference to the TV programme Sesame Street, obviously assuming that this programme is well-known
all over the world. This attempt fails, however, and the lecturer does not succeed
in making the students understand his intentions. We can only speculate about
the reasons: either the students are irritated by the sudden change of topic (from
PAH to Sesame Street), in particular, since the questions about PAH and about
Sesame Street show exactly the same syntactic structure. Another explanation
could be that the students indeed do not know Sesame Street or that this TV programme has country-specific variants. Nevertheless, as can be seen in Example
(4), the lecturer's advice to ask more questions seems to have had an effect.

Example (4): SOP

(*later on, in the same session*)
L: how do you learn about the machine?
S3:   read it in the guide?
L: what?
S3:   read it in the guide?
L: read it in the guard?
S3:   guide
L: oh yes (..) you read it in the SOP

S4:   (*very quickly*) what is SOP?

(*laughter*)

L: yes that is good you try to learn (...) standard operating procedure

Example (5): Latin

L: who of you knows Latin? (4.0) simile similem solvuntur
S1:   similar dissolves similar
S2:   similar dissolves similarly yeah
L: ja (-) similar dissolves similar (..) ok (...) so that is VEry true for liquid chromatography

Here again, as in Example (1), the lecturer tries to draw upon the students' knowledge of other languages which they might have at their disposal as a shared repertoire. Although two of the students respond to this strategy, one may wonder whether the reference to Latin has any significance for the Chinese students in the course.

Example (6): Rubin

L: that means this is here (---) a: ru rubin is rub
S1:   was ist rubin?
L: rubin is a crystal (---) it's a
S2:   rubin
S1:   the red?
S2:   yes
L: it's red
S1:   rubin yeah
L::   do you say rubin in English too?
S2:   rubin
L: ok (.) so that is a completely (-) spherical shaped rubin crystal (1.5) and it sits here (-) and it's used as a valve = so when we decrease the pressure in here solvent can be sucked into the piston chamber

In this extract, we have another example of a metalinguistic sequence in which the polysemy of *rubin* and parallels between English and German are discussed with the purpose of clarifying meaning.

Example (7): Grating and aperture

L: I always forget that word (-) what is a gitter?
Ss: grating (.) grid
L: grating (.) grid

S1:   grating

L: grating (--) ok we have a holographic grating here (.) and we SEParate into
       the different wave length (.) so we can separate into for example red green
       and the blue parts of the absorbance spectre and that resembles here a PART
       of a photo (unintelligible) ja?

S1:   whats Blende again?

L: what is Blende? = aPERture

S1:   lens

L: nee nee lens not

S1:   no?

L: aPERTure (1.0) bl it's the opening (---)

S1:   ah APerture

L: APerture ok

This example is similar to Example (2), since again the lecturer has some problems finding appropriate English words for expressing the intended meaning,
and again he gets support from a student. In the first case (grating) he accepts the
student's suggestion. In the second case (aperture), the lecturer offers a suggestion, which, however, is not accepted by S1 (because of the incorrect pronunciation, as it turns out later). S1 offers "lens" as an alternative, but the lecturer rejects
this, because, as it seems, he knows the meaning of "lens", which is not what he
intends to express. Only his paraphrase "opening" makes S1 aware of the lecturer's
deviant pronunciation of "aperture". Thus, in a joint endeavour, the lecturer and
S1 co-construct the appropriate solution to L's communication problem.

In summary, the following characteristics of lingua franca EMI interaction in
this course in Applied Chemistry can be stated:

Although some of the participants – including the lecturer – show deviations
from the syntax of Standard English rather frequently, this does not seem to affect
comprehensibility. In the occasional metalinguistic sequences of interaction (see
below) syntax is never focussed upon.

Pronunciation is seldom an issue. Only occasionally is it made a subject of
discussion.[6] It is notable, however, that this is mostly the case when the comprehension of lexical items is jeopardized (chelates vs. Kilos; guide vs. guard;

---

6.   Although this cannot be seen from the examples presented in this article, there is, however,
one student in the group whose utterances are often unintelligible. The lecturer sometimes
reacts with "I had difficulties to understand you – once more, please" or "as far as I understand
you". In these cases transcription of this student's utterances was sometimes impossible, and the
research assistant who recorded the data noted down that this student's accent had a negative
effect on intelligibility.

aperture). The lecturer himself plays down the importance of "correct" pronunciation: "We don't care about pronunciation" (Example (1)).

The focus is clearly on the comprehension of the meaning of lexical items and on finding the appropriate English word for expressing intended meanings: "do you say shovel?" (Example (2)), "What is Schablone auf Englisch"? (Example (2)), "Ditches – do you say that? Oh, my English is so bad" (Example (2)), "do you say rubin in English too?" (Example (6)). Often initiated by the lecturer himself, participants cooperate in the construction and the expression of meaning by trying to agree on an appropriate lexical item or to explain its meaning. (e.g. Example (7)).

Whereas the students' problems with lexical items mainly refer to subject-specific scientific terminology, the lecturer's lexical problems are of a different nature. While students have to struggle with scientific terms like phenanthroline, the lecturer is at a loss when it comes to shovels and ditches. Characteristics of his teaching style seem to be responsible for this: he has the habit of switching from theoretical explanations to descriptions of objects and activities from everyday life, and back again. He talks about crabs, claws, shovels, ditches and Sesame Street in a lecture on Applied Chemistry – and this is exactly where he encounters lexical problems. The use of everyday language fulfils several functions in his teaching: the function of metaphor (crab, claw), the function of describing applications of chemistry (shovels, ditches), and the function of influencing the participants' communicative behaviour by making reference to (assumed) shared cultural background knowledge (Sesame Street).

The lecturer makes use of several strategies to ensure comprehension.

Firstly, he does not try to avoid topics and – as a consequence – sequences of discourse that the lexical component of his learner language is not able to deal with. This, however, may contribute to the students' deeper understanding of the contents of the seminar and may also support the retention of terms and their underlying concepts. In doing so, he does not try to conceal the inadequacies of his learner language, and there is no indication that he regards this as face threatening in any way. Several times he asks explicitly for the English translation of a German word – a strategy that can, however, only work because he is assisted by the only native speaker of English in the group, who has also a good command of German and who acts as an interpreter/translator. The relaxed way in which the lecturer handles his problems with the English language is typical of a type 1 set-up, as defined above: there is no intention on part of the lecturer to teach the English language beyond subject-specific terminology or to be something like a 'perfect model'. Any further improvement of the students' competence in the English language happens just incidentally. This is in sharp contrast to type 2 set-ups and particularly so in courses in English linguistics and literature, where the lecturer is supposed to be an expert on English with the additional goal of enhancing the students' general competence in the English language.

Secondly, the lecturer uses comprehension checks frequently and he encourages the students to make clarification requests (Example (3)).

Noticeably, the lecturer draws on all the linguistic resources available (or assumed to be available) in the group, above all the native speaker of English with her additional competence in the German language, but also on the other students' competence in the English language, the Macedonian student's linguistic background, and even Latin and Greek. In doing so, he often initiates metalinguistic detours from the subject under discussion in order to clarify meaning.

The lecturer does not put any pressure on the students to speak "correct English", as long as intelligibility and comprehensibility are not affected negatively.

The many instances of laughter as well as the humorous stretches of discourse which some of the students join in at times suggest that the lecturer has succeeded in creating a relaxed atmosphere and making students feel comfortable.

5.   Some consequences

In spite of the small-scale character of the studies presented in this article, the results suggest some theoretical as well as practical consequences. Some of these refer to the conceptualisation of lingua franca discourse and of EMI. Lingua franca as well as EMI discourse come in a variety of formats. Sometimes EMI is lingua franca discourse (with varying degrees of 'lingua-francaness'), sometimes it is not. Some of the other relevant parameters of variation are genre of discourse, number of participants, variety and common ground in the linguistic resources available, the interactional goals and the institutional or non-institutional framing of the interaction.

Instructional discourse with English as a medium of instruction for non-native speakers of English is characterised by specific combinations of these variables and therefore needs to be a special object of research. In particular, we need more insights into how EMI affects teaching styles and learning results at university. Studies from the CLIL context at school, still inconclusive in themselves, can only serve as rough guidelines here, since the university situation differs from the school situation in many respects: in school contexts there is usually a lower degree of 'lingua-francaness', i.e., normally most participants share the same L1. The size of groups is much more variable at university, and participants have less of a common history of interaction. Moreover, university lecturers with an expertise in multilingualism or foreign language teaching and with an awareness of how language choice may influence teaching and learning are rather the exception than the rule.

Last but not least, those who are responsible for setting up international university programmes and those who decide upon the language of instruction in universities should make wise and informed decisions and offer appropriate support to make the best of EMI, where it is considered to be useful and reasonable.

References

Ammon, U. & McConnell, G. 2002. *English as an Academic Language in Europe: A Survey of its Use in Teaching.* Frankfurt: Peter Lang.

Ammon, U. 1998. *Ist Deutsch noch internationale Wissenschaftssprache? Englisch auch für die Lehre an deutschsprachigen Hochschulen.* Berlin: de Gruyter.

Ammon, U. 2006. Language planning for international scientific communication. *Current Issues in Language Planning* 7: 1–30.

Carli, A. & Ammon, U. 2007. *Linguistic Inequality in Scientific Communication Today. What can Future Applied Linguistics do to Mitigate Disadvantages for Non-anglophones?* [*AILA Review* 20]. Amsterdam: John Benjamins.

Clyne, M. G. 1984. *Language and Society in the German Speaking Countries.* Cambridge: CUP.

Coleman, J. A. 2006. English-medium teaching in European Higher Education. *Language Teaching* 39(1): 1–14.

DAAD (Deutscher Akademischer Austauschdienst) (ed.). 2009. *Daten und Fakten zur Internationalisierung von Studium und Forschung in Deutschland.* Bielefeld: Bertelsmann. <www.wissenschaft-weltoffen.de/daten>.

Ehlich, K. 2000. Deutsch als Wissenschaftssprache für das 21. Jahrhundert. *German as a Foreign Language* 1. <http://www.gfl-journal.com>.

Ehlich, K. 2005. Deutsch als Medium wissenschaftlichen Arbeitens. In *Englisch oder Deutsch in Internationalen Studiengängen?*, M. Motz (ed.), 41–51. Frankfurt: Peter Lang.

Firth, A. 1996. The discursive accomplishment of normality: On 'Lingua Franca' English and conversational analysis. *Journal of Pragmatics* 26: 237–259.

Graddol, D. 1997. *The Future of English?* London: British Council.

Hellekjaer, G. 2004. Unprepared for English-medium instruction. A critical look at beginner students. In *Integrating Content and Language. Meeting the Challenge of a Multilingual Higher Education*, R. Wilkinson (ed.), 147–161. Maastricht: Universitaire Pers Maastricht.

Knapp, A. & Münch, A. 2008. Doppelter Lernaufwand? Deutsche Studierende in englischsprachigen Lehrveranstaltungen. In *Mehrsprachigkeit und Multikulturalität im Studium*, A. Knapp & A. Schumann (eds), 171–196. Frankfurt: Peter Lang.

Knapp, K. & Meierkord, C. (eds). 2002. *Lingua Franca Communication.* Frankfurt: Peter Lang.

Marsh, D. & Wolff, D. (eds). 2007. *Diverse Contexts- Converging Goals: CLIL in Europe.* Frankfurt: Peter Lang.

Mauranen, A. & Ranta, E. (eds). 2009. *English as a Lingua Franca: Studies and Findings.* Newcastle upon Tyne: Cambridge Scholars Publishing.

Snow Andrade, M. 2006. International students in English-speaking universities: Adjustment factors. *Journal of Research in International Education* 5: 131–154.

Varghese, N. 2008. *Globalization of Higher Education and Cross-Border Student Mobility*. Research papers IIEP. Paris: International Institute for Educational Planning.

Vollmer, H. J. 2005. Bilingualer Sachfachunterricht als Inhalts- und als Sprachenlernen. In *Bilingualer Unterricht. Grundlagen, Methoden, Praxis, Perspektiven*, G. Bach & S. Niemeier (eds), 47–70. Frankfurt: Peter Lang.

Wächter, B. & Maiworm, F. 2008. *English-Taught Programmes in European Higher Education. The Picture in 2007*. Bonn: Lemmens.

Wolff, D. 2009. Content and language integrated learning. In *Handbook of Foreign Language Learning and Communication*, K. Knapp & B. Seidlhofer (eds), 545–572. Berlin: de Gruyter.

English as a *lingua franca* and the Standard English misunderstanding

Kurt Kohn
University of Tübingen, Germany

This article adopts a social constructivist and developmental perspective on English as a *lingua franca* (ELF). On this basis and with reference to the *My English* condition, it explores the conflict generally perceived between non-native speaker-learners' claim of ownership of English and their preference for Standard English target models. The conflict is shown to result from a conceptual misunderstanding caused by the conflation of Standard English as an object of linguistic description and Standard English as a cognitive, emotional and social construct by the speaker-learners themselves. With the constructivist reconciliation of ownership and target language preference, the role of Standard English in second language learning and teaching appears in a new and refreshing light.

Karlfried Knapp is one of my oldest colleagues and friends in applied linguistics. Not long after our earlier years in the field of contrastive analysis, he began blazing trails into the new territories of intercultural communication (Knapp, Enninger & Knapp-Potthoff 1987) and English as a lingua franca (Knapp 1987). He had thus been long around when I joined in many years later – just in time to honour him with this contribution.

Struggling towards ownership

English enables non-native speakers to gain access to a globalised world of communication and to overcome barriers of language and culture. But more often than not they are also forced to hide their intellectual and communicative capabilities under a bushel, while native speakers can be quite carefree about how they exploit and display their 'home field' advantage. The following mail dialog took place in the mail forum of the IATEFL LT SIG[1] (29 April 2005, message 1290) after the webmaster (WM) had corrected a website mistake that had been brought to his attention by a visitor:

> WM: "I believe every instance of this slip [i.e. the website mistake] has now been apprehended and marched off for corrective discipline, but should you happen to spot any stray infelicities wandering vaguely in the backwaters, I'd be obliged if you'd let me know."
>
> Visitor: "Not a huge disaster, I don't think. Thanks for spotting it and sorting it out with such alacrity. And for the delightful sentence."

This is amusing banter between two native speakers who seem to be in their own world rather than in an international forum. While their exchange might have been stimulating and instructive for some non-native speakers in the mail forum, it might have been discouraging for others, making them feel even clumsier than usual and reluctant to participate in the discussion.

It is not always easy these days for non-native speakers of English to find their place of identity in the English-speaking world. Torn between seemingly conflicting needs and requirements regarding communication, communal participation, self-image and esteem, knowing and learning, non-native speakers sometimes find it hard to feel at ease with themselves and to perform at the top of their potential (cf. Albl-Mikasa 2009; Knapp 2002). But compare Ehrenreich's (2009: 139) observations about "the self-confident and efficient" use of ELF in business contexts (see also Seidlhofer, this volume).

Non-native speakers on the rise

This is all the more frustrating since out there in real life, non-native speakers are on the rise. In Europe and around the world they are increasing in numbers, using their own version(s) of English for their own authentic communication purposes. Against this backdrop, researchers have convincingly – and encouragingly – argued in favour of the non-native speakers' right to ownership of English. "Native speakers may feel the language 'belongs' to them, but it will be those who speak English as a second or foreign language who will determine its world future" (Graddol 1997: 10). This is a descriptive statement, not a normative one. The development of a language is *de facto* a matter of those people who use it for their communicative needs and purposes. In the case of an international language

---

1. International Association of Teachers of English as a Foreign Language (IATEFL) – Learning Technologies Special Interest Group.

like English, this inevitably includes its non-native speakers. From an empirical-descriptive perspective, native speakers contribute to the development of English through their communicative involvement, but they do not possess privileged rights as natural guardians.

> How English develops in the world is no business whatever of native speakers in England, the United States, or anywhere else. They have no say in the matter, no right to intervene or pass judgement. They are irrelevant. The very fact that English is an international language means that no nation can have custody over it. To grant such custody over the language is necessarily to arrest its development and so undermine its international status.   (Widdowson 2003: 43)

All this is evidence of changes in language awareness shaped by descriptive observation, rather than prescriptive values and preferences of native speaker-centered foreign language pedagogy. Kachru's (1985) original plea for more sociolinguistic realism regarding the norm developing for speakers of English as a second language in so-called outer circle countries like India is now being extended to include all non-native speakers who use English in natural, real-life communication contexts.

Owning a house is one thing; however, making it one's home is yet another. If non-native speakers accept ownership, they also need to begin to feel responsible for themselves. Before being able to shape the future of English, they need to get their own English into shape. But which direction should they take? Does ownership require them to leave the familiar grounds of foreign language learning and to let go of Standard English as a learning target, and of native speakers as role models? The situation is far less clear than it used to be.

Crumbling authorities

Native speakers are losing their status as beacons of orientation. Their decline has been described in both quantitative and qualitative terms (Graddol 1999). Thus, the sheer number of native speakers of English relative to the number of non-native speakers is decreasing. At the same time, the shares of non-native speakers in world-wide communication have gone up. But more important than numbers are the qualitative changes that go hand in hand with the functional shift from learning English as a foreign language (EFL) to using English as a lingua franca (ELF) in multilingual and multicultural contexts. And what is more, being immersed in real and relevant communicative interaction, not only with native speakers but increasingly with other non-native speakers, leads to changing perceptions of oneself, and of what knowing and using English is all about.

It hardly comes as a surprise that these changes in communicative practice, needs and attitudes are also reflected in language pedagogy. Until fairly recently, the target role of native speaker English was hardly contested. And even in a global context, this position seems to prevail, as can be witnessed in David Crystal's (2003) appraisal of his own native English:

> In my ideal world, everyone would have fluent command of a single world language. I am already in the fortunate position of being a fluent user of the language which is most in contention for this role, and have cause to reflect every day on the benefits of having it at my disposal.   (p. xiii)

The pedagogic implication of this sigh of contentment is only too clear: learn (and teach) native speaker English and you will become part of the speech community on which the sun never sets. A somewhat sobering counterpoint is set by David Graddol (2006). In his analysis of the demographic, economic, technological, societal and linguistic forces under which English is currently developing to take on a more global form, he predicts the end of orthodox foreign language teaching approaches and questions the pedagogic usefulness of native-speaker models:

> In the new rapidly emerging climate, native speakers may increasingly be identified as a part of the problem rather than the source of solution. They may be seen as bringing with them cultural baggage in which learners wanting to use English primarily as an international language are not interested.   (p. 114)

In this view, native speakers are being downgraded from embodying a "gold standard" and being the "final arbiters of quality and authority" (p. 114) to an obstacle for both learning and communication. Also, resources of authentic native-speaker usage might be helpful for native speaker education but not for international non-native learners of English (p. 115).

Pragmatic and sociocultural studies of language learning and communication help to better convey the reasoning underlying the pedagogic devaluation of the native speaker. Considering what is known about second and bilingual language learning, it is not very realistic to expect non-native learners to acquire "the same mastery over a language as an (educated) native speaker" (Byram 1997: 21) on all levels of grammatical, lexical and sociocultural competence. And what is more, pushing learners towards native speaker proficiency means pushing them towards "a native sociocultural competence, and a new sociocultural identity" (Byram 1997: 11) which is not their own.

This sociocultural foreignness, which is inherent in a native-speaker model, becomes even more noticeable with Widdowson's terminological distinction between discourse and text. Discourse is "the pragmatic process of meaning negotiation" (2004: 8) we engage in when we communicate with each other; text is the linguistic product or manifestation of this process. The relationship between the two is neither fixed nor predictable. On the one hand, a text is designed (by the producer) to facilitate the realisation (by the recipient) of certain discourse intentions; on the other hand, however, the unfolding discourse is always underdetermined by the linguistic means of expression used in the text. Interpreting a text, i.e., authenticating it as a particular kind of discourse, necessarily and inevitably requires readers to reach out beyond the text itself into their sociocultural conceptualizations of reality.

Text-based communication thus requires lexical and grammatical knowledge – but it is always knowledge geared to meet the speakers' discourse-related sociocultural requirements and needs. It is in this sociocultural dimension that things are usually quite different between native and non-native speakers of English. While learning a new language certainly also provides the opportunity to gain access to a new sociocultural community of discourse and communication, it must be doubted whether exposure to a native-speaker model is the most suitable approach for most non-native learners of English. It might be too demanding for no justifiable reasons; or it might be just inappropriate for the learner's own communicative and communal discourse needs and purposes.

The native speaker concept has come under attack from an empirical perspective as well. On closer inspection, key assumptions regarding expertise, authority and consistency cannot be supported. Any questions about 'the' native speaker's grammatical knowledge or preferences of usage inevitably lead to 'real' native speakers and a heterogeneous display of socioculturally shaped variation. "In other words, the abstract concept of the native speaker ceases to be useful as soon as we try to extract descriptive details from it" (Leung 2005: 130). Because of this high degree of abstraction, the native speaker concept is particularly susceptible to prescriptive generalizations presented in the guise of description with little or no hard empirical evidence.

A similar combination of empirical abstraction and prescriptive idealization characterizes the notion of Standard English. For "self-elected members of a rather exclusive club", it is a convenient vehicle for promoting a particular brand of 'native speaker' variety as "socially sanctioned for institutional use" and for presenting its extensive descriptions as a specification of "what is acceptable as proper English and what is not" (Widdowson 2003: 37).

Standard English is thus seen as a form of English which enjoys high social value and which needs to be protected to keep the English language from falling apart into myriads of varieties within the native speaker countries and around the world. In this vein, Quirk (1985: 6) states that the "relatively narrow range of purposes for which the non-native needs to use English [...] is arguably well catered for by a single monochrome standard form that looks as good on paper as it sounds in speech". Clearly, in his view, the promotion of Standard English does not include non-native ownership. With non-native speakers on the loose, as it were, a non-standard Babel threatens to become reality (cf. Quirk 1990; but compare the criticism in Kachru 1991). Quirk's position is countered by Jenkins' (2007) empirical investigation of a "Standard English ideology" in the language teaching profession. She hypothesizes this ideology to be at work in various instances of a Standard English preference and suspects it to stifle all ELF development and emancipation.

New complexities

Where does this leave the non-native speaker? A once clearly laid out English speaking world with unambiguous do's and don'ts has become less transparent and less predictable – but at the same time richer and more demanding, with interesting possibilities and challenges for the enterprising non-native speaker. This new complexity is also evident in English language pedagogy: Standard English still enjoys a privileged status – yet, the empire is crumbling and educational standards, curriculum descriptions and teaching practices are slowly being modified under the influence of the changes that take place in the real world of English communication.

In German secondary schools, for instance, the situation appears to be creatively inconsistent (cf. Kohn 2007). On the one hand, Standard English (in its British or American versions) remains the proclaimed target norm. On the other hand, however, non-native teachers and (new) correction rules that favour communicative skills over form add a certain touch of 'freedom'. At the same time, the educational authorities are beginning to take notice of pupils' needs regarding the use of English in lingua franca and intercultural contact situations. While the signals are still weak, they mark a shift away from the exclusive native speaker focus of the traditional foreign language teaching dogma and open a door for the development and implementation of more realistic pedagogical approaches. In addition, with the promotion of early foreign language learning and content and language integrated learning (CLIL), new contexts and conditions for classroom interaction are being introduced which strengthen and authenticate the overall communicative orientation and arguably lead to a cautious relaxation of Standard English norms.

At German universities this leads to a certain discrepancy between teaching and real communication. Language teachers are generally required to be native speakers and Standard English provides the target model. However, globalization trends in higher education and student mobility across Europe are favouring the

'Englishization' of certain study programmes. This increasingly results in courses being offered in English by non-native lecturers and in students being immersed in multilingual academic and private contact situations with English as a lingua franca (see also Seidlhofer, this volume). The native speaker requirement also holds for English language teachers/trainers in business and vocational contexts – but with a more relaxed focus on Standard English. Communication comes before form; and English as a lingua franca (ELF) is seen as an advantage rather than a threat (cf. Ehrenreich 2009; Graddol 2006).

Throughout school, university and work environment, European non-native speakers of English are thus moving in a complex matrix of seemingly conflicting linguistic, communicative, sociocultural and pedagogic principles, needs and challenges. Traditionally familiar pillars of security, which non-native speakers were accustomed to lean on, are giving way to a cacophony of possibilities. The non-native speaker's perception of non-native English is marked by variety and differences: differences between school and real life, between ELF in academia, business, trade, and on the shop floor, between countries and global regions, between non-native speakers of different learning and teaching backgrounds and levels of proficiency – all contributing to surface manifestations, which lead James (2005) to characterize ELF as an "instance of language in a postmodern world. It is fragmented, contingent, marginal, transitional, indeterminate, ambivalent and hybrid in various ways" (p. 141).

The need for ELF analyses

From early on, researchers have called for empirical studies to describe what is possible and appropriate in ELF (cf. Seidlhofer 2001, 2005).

Corpora and corpus techniques play a key role in the endeavour to collect and analyse relevant data on a larger scale. VOICE, the Vienna-Oxford International Corpus of English, comprises transcribed recordings of ELF interactions that cover different genres of spoken discourse and come from a wide range of first language backgrounds and communicative settings. The VOICE data are available online and, along with the online VOICE search and analysis tools, provide a rich basis for studying lexical, grammatical and pragmatic characteristics of ELF (cf. Klimpfinger 2009; Pitzl 2009; Seidlhofer 2009; Seidlhofer, Breiteneder & Pitzl 2006). In the ELFA corpus the focus is on monologic and dialogic/polylogic spoken ELF interactions in academic settings (cf. Mauranen 2009; Mauranen 2010; Mauranen, Hynninen & Ranta 2010). The ELFA data are made available to researchers on request.

A somewhat different approach is pursued with the small Tübingen English as a Lingua Franca (TELF) corpus. The objective of the TELF project is to enrich the textual manifestation of ELF interactions with introspective data specifically geared to facilitate insights into the problems, forces and strategic processes that are at work behind the scene. For this purpose, the TELF corpus approach combines three types of data: video-recorded ELF discussions in mixed groups of four to six native and non-native speakers of English from diverse linguistic and cultural backgrounds, interviews with the speakers about their developmental history and performance requirements, and retrospective speaker comments about selected discussion passages and phenomena (cf. Albl-Mikasa 2009).

Complementary to descriptions based on corpora like VOICE, ELFA or TELF, Wenger's (1998) notion of "community of practice" (CofP) has been proposed for studying emerging attitudes, strategies and conventions characteristic of ELF communication (cf. Jenkins 2007; Knapp 2009; Seidlhofer 2007, 2009). The descriptive and explanatory value of the CofP approach has been convincingly demonstrated by preliminary findings available from ELF interactions in two multinational corporations in Germany (cf. Ehrenreich 2009).

Insights from both corpus analyses and CofP studies are required for helping us work out principles, task designs and materials for an English language pedagogy that incorporates non-native speakers' ownership of English as a viable and necessary teaching and learning objective. Empirical studies, however, the data they are based on and the conclusions that are drawn from them, never come 'naked'. They are crucially dependent on models and on the concepts and assumptions upon which they are based and that are more or less taken for granted. To further prepare the ground for our discussion of ELF and the issue of a non-native speaker's ownership of English, it is thus necessary now to take a closer look at models and to clarify how we want to think and talk about ELF.

A developmental perspective

The *My English* condition

According to a prototypical definition, ELF is "a common language between persons not sharing any other language for communication purposes and not having English as their primary language" (James 2005: 134). But how can we conceptualize this common language?

From a sociolinguistic perspective, a suitable candidate would be one of the (many) Englishes ELF speakers are exposed to – or rather the virtual language (cf. Widdowson 2003: 48pp.) behind the scene – and which, in the course of ELF communication, they manage to appropriate for ELF tasks and purposes. This also seems to be the understanding that underlies most current research studies focusing on how English is *used as* a lingua franca (cf. Mauranen & Ranta 2009).

For my own theoretical and empirical orientation in ELF research, I would like to add a further model dimension, that of social construction (cf. Vygotsky 1978). According to this model, all perception, learning, action and communication is the result of individual processes of cognitive (and emotional) construction, overlaid and shaped by collaboration in social groups. This perspective allows for an even more comprehensive approach in that it offers a unified basis for investigating the entire heterogeneous range of non-native speaker manifestations of English, including ELF manifestations by speakers with an EFL background. It also provides a methodological framework in which it is possible to include and analyse ELF contributions by native speakers of English.

Conceptualizing 'English as a lingua franca' from a social constructivist perspective has interesting implications for the perennial question of which language a group of people agree to speak in a multilingual communicative situation when they say: "Let's talk English". Is it the English of native speakers? Is it some kind of Standard English: Quirk's "monochrome standard form" (1985: 6) or Crystal's "World Standard Spoken English" (2003: 185ff.)? Is it a non-native speaker ELF variety? Or is it something entirely different? A little thought experiment might help to illuminate the issue (cf. Kohn 2007). Let us suppose members of a European project meet for the first time. The question of a common project language is brought up, and the following exchange takes place:

(1)   – *Well, although Ryan is the only English native speaker in our group, I propose English as our lingua franca.*
      – *That's fine with me. My company is operating internationally and English is our main working language anyway.*
      – *Okay. That gives me the opportunity to practise my school English.*
      – *Ehm, my English not good but I manage.*

Quite obviously, the project members are not proposing to use some native speaker standard or a particular non-native speaker ELF variety. They are inevitably following the social constructivist *My English* condition according to which each speaker can only use his or her own individual English, i.e., the version of English they have managed to *make their own* – be this as a consolidated, stable and highly differentiated *native language*, a consolidated and stable but somewhat restricted *second language*, or as a reduced and unstable *learner's language*. This is the only option available to them; and they all assume (or hope) that in this way they will be able to communicate successfully.

And how do people make English their own? The answer is deceptively simple: *they acquire it*. But rather than like acquiring a car or a house, people acquire English, or any other language, by creatively constructing their own version of it in their minds, hearts and behaviour. This process of constructing one's language is influenced by a number of factors as, for example, target language orientation, exposure to various manifestations of English in pedagogic contexts or in natural (ELF) communication, mother tongue(s), attitudes and motivation, goals and requirements, learning approaches taken, and effort invested. But none of these factors *determines* the outcome. Acquiring a language is the very opposite of copying or cloning – it is a cognitive and emotional process of sociocultural and communicative construction. Making a language one's own thus necessarily involves creative change and development (see also Widdowson 2003: 50pp.; Seidlhofer & Widdowson 2009). Regardless of how powerful the communicative and communal pull towards a 'common core' might be, the English that people develop is inevitably different from any target language model they chose or were forced to adopt.

Developing *My English*

The *My English* condition emphasizes the developmental perspective incorporated in the ownership issue. The English we observe in ELF situations only exists insofar as its speakers have acquired and developed it, i.e., insofar as its speakers have also been – and usually still are – *learners of English* in the broadest sense. Language learning is thus an inevitable and necessary condition of ELF. Trying to understand the nature of English in ELF situations should therefore be extended to also include its developmental matrix. Despite the criticism voiced by Jenkins (2006), I wish to emphasize that ELF and second language acquisition (SLA) research should be seen as brothers in arms working on different, yet complementary sections of the same empirical continuum. This is not to claim that just any contribution from SLA research is relevant or helpful for understanding ELF. Quite the contrary. Incorporating a developmental perspective into the modelling and analysis of ELF will no doubt bring about a fresh look at empirical and methodological issues in SLA research as well (cf. Canagarajah 2007).

For my own line of argumentation in this article, I would like to focus now on one particular aspect of language learning and development, namely the nature of what is involved in developing *My English*.

First of all, developing *My English* is about developing my linguistic knowledge of phonetic-phonological, lexical and grammatical means of expression. However, since this is not knowledge separate from real life, but rather knowledge designed to serve my communicative needs and purposes, it includes knowing how these linguistic means of expression can be used to fulfil my own self-imposed communication and community-oriented requirements of performance (cf. Kohn 1990). Such requirements concern in particular comprehensibility and self-expression, compliance with a target language model (which is not necessarily Standard English), regarding grammatical accuracy and situational appropriateness, participation in a speech fellowship, or expression of my self.

But developing *My English* is also about developing requirements of performance. In first language acquisition, for instance, little children develop their native language with an almost exclusive initial focus on comprehension. It is only gradually and in connection with their growing sense of community that requirements concerning accuracy become relevant for them as well. These become more refined over the years. Creating their language thus goes hand in hand with creating and cultivating their own requirements of performance. The same holds for immigrants in second language acquisition settings. On which level their language acquisition stops is largely influenced by the socio-psychological development of their requirement profile. In this connection, compare Schumann's (1978) reference to a pidginization process or Selinker's fossilization hypothesis (cf. Selinker & Lamendella 1980). The situation is somewhat different for traditional foreign language learners who have developed their requirements of performance mainly in dissociation from communicative needs and feelings of communal belonging. In this case, a requirement of correctness in the sense of norm compliance and enforcement is more or less dominant, which usually is an obstacle for natural communication, inhibiting speakers from opening their mouths unless they feel entirely sure they are correct. Extended communicative exposure under lingua franca conditions may then lead to a more differentiated and 'liberated' requirement profile with new options for ELF performance.

Finally, developing *My English* is about developing the speaker-learners' sense and desire for identification and participation with certain speech communities, which then shows up in their requirement profiles and eventually in their own performance. The children in first language acquisition settings and the immigrants in second language acquisition settings mentioned above serve to illustrate this point. In school education, a year abroad often – and hopefully – leads to new communal alliances with accompanying changes in the pupils' requirements of performance. While this usually leaves positive traces in the pupils' communicative competence, it might also bring them in partial conflict with more traditionally minded teachers. Conflicts due to diverging requirements of performance can thus arise between successful communicative participation in a particular native speaker or ELF community on the one hand, and successful participation in a pedagogic community on the other hand. But conflicts can also happen when speakers move across and between different ELF communities characterized by different requirements.

The requirement profile that a speaker has developed (and is developing) in relation to a particular language is shaped by the sociocultural, pedagogic and personal conditions in which he or she has acquired and used (is acquiring and using) this language. It should be noted, however, that as regards its activation in communication, a requirement profile is not fixed and rigid but usually rather sensitive to situational factors. While in some situations it might be of primary importance to meet the requirement of comprehensibility, giving appropriate communal signals might be more important in others. In their communicative performance, speakers thus try to strategically monitor their utterances with regard to their own requirements. That is, they intentionally use certain means of expression *in order to* comply with specific requirements. This is possible precisely because their linguistic knowledge is not just knowledge of phonetic-phonological, lexical and grammatical means of expression; it is in fact knowledge about how and to what extent requirements of performance can be fulfilled with which linguistic means.

Usually, speakers are more or less conscious of the requirements of performance that are in force for them, and they are quite able to give explicit judgments regarding their requirement profile and how well it is met by their performance. The following data are taken from an earlier study on the strategic dimension of second language acquisition (Kohn 1990: Chapter 5). Speakers were non-native exchange students in the United States, who were as much learners of English as they were users of English in natural communication with native speakers and other non-native speakers:

> S1: "[…] and maybe funny for them. My grammar and writing is better than a speaking and listening. When I a speaking and interview with a person sometimes I ashame […] When I speak correct I am happy and when I have mistake is very bad. Maybe think I am illiteracy."
>
> S2: "Only important thing is the people understand me when I speak; but not it's necessary to speak correctly. […] If I want to speak correctly, like now [i.e., in the interview], I must thinking, thinking and I don't like it. I can speak only – I like to speak rapidly."

These statements reflect the speakers' requirement profiles and, what is particularly important in our context, an interesting tension between teaching/learning-related and communication-related requirements. The speakers are clearly striving to reach a balance between sociocultural and linguistic norms and conventions suggested or even enforced on them from the outside, and their own needs and preferences. Similar statements can be found in the TELF corpus:

S3: "I actually aim at a high standard English. I have to pass exams. I will be a teacher so it has to be a good level. [...] I prefer American English, it's easier for me to understand."

S4: "I'd like to aim at perfection, but I'm far away from it, erm, from it, sorry, so, well, I'm aiming to, erm, to can speak fl..., erm, to be able to speak fluently and, erm, to understand fluent English spoken at me."

S5: "I basically aim for fluency and to be able to express myself clearly so my audience would be able to pick what I'm saying."

Again, the speakers have fairly differentiated requirement profiles, which reflect not only their teaching background and learning history, but also their future goals, communicative needs and personal preferences. At the same time, it is evident that having a certain requirement does not necessarily mean it can be easily achieved.

Target orientation

In the empirical studies mentioned above many subjects talk quite naturally about their requirement of correctness. Considering the widespread native speaker and Standard English orientation in the non-native speaker world, this is hardly surprising. But what is the status of a requirement of correctness in the ELF context? First, it can be safely acknowledged that the notion of correctness, in one way or another, forms part of many, if not most, non-native ELF speakers' realities. This holds in particular if we accept a social constructivist model approach to ELF, which also includes ELF speakers with a foreign language learning background. Second, it is important to note that 'correctness' is a coin with two sides. The term is commonly used to refer to a relation between a learner's products of performance (often taken as evidence of underlying competence) and an external standard norm. This is a common view which has its roots in the (behaviourist-structuralist) contrastive analysis approach with its assumptions about imitation and transfer, and in the identification of errors as deviations from the target language. Also, it has kept a strong presence in the further development of second language acquisition research. From error (Corder 1967) and interlanguage analysis (Selinker 1972) to the analysis of learner strategies (Færch & Kasper 1983) and the study of pushed output processing (Swain 1985, 1995, 2005), language learning is being seen as a process that moves towards the language spoken by native speakers. It is a view which has been facilitated by a long-standing focus on grammar, and on getting things right or wrong – even in communicatively-oriented approaches (cf. Canale & Swain 1980).

On closer inspection, however, the external view on correctness and errors falls short of explaining what non-native speaker-learners are doing and why. According to the social constructivist *My English* condition, correctness and errors also need to be seen from an internal perspective. No external factors are able to influence a person's performance and learning unless they are given some kind of internal, cognitive-emotional representation. The very best that non-native speaker-learners who want to be correct can do is to use those forms they *feel* are correct. Whether these forms are truly correct compared to an external standard norm is quite a different matter. Standard English and native speaker English can thus only serve as models and provide orientation for non-native speaker-learners' performance and learning in so far as they have gained a second existence in the speaker-learners' internally constructed world. But this internal construction is not just a mirror image of the external 'thing'; it is the result of processes that feed on intake from external data and, not less importantly, on knowledge, attitudes and interests already available.

Regarding standard native speaker English, there is thus a fundamental difference between what linguists (i.e., experts) aim to capture in their descriptive constructions and what non-native speaker-learners (i.e., laypersons) have internalised as beacons of orientation. A non-native speaker-learner's internal construction of, say, Mid-Atlantic Standard English might be the typically sketchy, heterogeneous, messy and unreliable product of accidental encounters and subjective interpretations, or it might be more systematic due to pedagogic mediation, and even based on linguistic description. But it does *not* aim to be a linguistic description itself. The problems and deficits that linguists identify with regard to over-abstraction, inconsistency and lack of sound empirical evidence belong to the linguists' world – they are irrelevant for the non-native speaker-learner. For this reason, all *descriptive-linguistic* arguments levelled against the *pedagogic* deployment of the notions of Standard English and native speaker English are based on a conceptual misunderstanding and simply miss their target.

From a social constructivist acquisition perspective, Standard English and native speaker English are thus perfectly compatible with non-native aspirations to ownership of English. Ownership is manifested in the English that speaker-learners develop and speak – but ownership already begins with how they construct English as a target model for their own learning. Whether Standard English has empirically valid manifestations in existing speech communities (or not) is for descriptive linguists to investigate; what counts in the process of learning, however, is the learners' own perceptual construction of Standard English. The claim of non-native speaker ownership and a pedagogical preference for Standard English as a target model are thus not at all in conflict. However, whether some kind of standard and native speaker English *should* be a pedagogic target model or not is a language political and educational issue which needs to be discussed in relation to the respective sociocultural context.

Pedagogic implications

EFL – the foreign language perspective

Among foreign languages in German schools, English is in first place. The curriculum regulations generally emphasize a communicative orientation with reference to the Common European Framework of Reference for Languages (Council of Europe 2001). The overall learning objective is to prepare pupils for language and communication requirements set by a globalized world of international cooperation and intercultural contact in which English serves as a global lingua franca. The Educational Standards for schools in the province of Baden-Württemberg (Landesbildungsserver 2004), for instance, describe the relevant target competences for 10th grade (sixth year of English; typically, students are 15 or 16 years old) on five dimensions: "kommunikative Fertigkeiten", "Beherrschung der sprachlichen Mittel", "Umgang mit Texten", "kulturelle Kompetenz", and "Methodenkompetenz".[2] The descriptions are characterized by a strong native speaker bias. Pupils are expected to understand national and regional pronunciations, clearly pronounced everyday conversations between native speakers, selected radio/TV broadcast and movies as well as less challenging newspaper articles and literary texts. In their own productions, pupils should be idiomatic in their word choice, and they should be able to pay attention to relevant differences between *BBC English* and *General American English*. Their utterances are required to be grammatically correct without too many interferences from German and only few errors that could cause misunderstandings. Their pronunciation should approximate the norms of *BBC English* or *General American English*. Formal and informal expressions should be used appropriately. Regarding, for example, politeness, greetings, or eating habits, pupils are expected to behave in culturally adequate ways according to British or American conventions. All in all, these target competences clearly focus on Standard English in the sense of a set of idealized native speaker norms of linguistic and cultural behaviour. The communicative acid test is contact with native speakers. Exposure to materials extracted from native speaker communication is also critical; whether pupils are able to authenticate these materials for themselves is a different matter.

---

2. Communicative skills, mastery of linguistic means of expression, dealing with texts, cultural competence, and methodological competence.

Except in the introductory statement, ELF and ELF-specific conditions of communication are not referred to in the Educational Standards for schools in the province of Baden-Württemberg, nor are possible pedagogic measures. The 11th grade curriculum introduces ELF as a special course subject: processes of globalization, Englishes around the world, and issues of linguistic imperialism. However, when it comes to language and communication-related learning objectives, ELF is again missing. The only venture outside native speaker communities is mentioned under the heading of intercultural competence and concerns the pupils' ability to cope with complex everyday situations involving second language varieties of English from outer circle countries like India.

ELF – the lingua franca perspective

What are the pedagogic challenges that follow from English being increasingly used as a European and global lingua franca and from the theoretical and empirical insights ELF research provides?

First of all, pupils should *know about ELF*. Relevant learning objectives in particular concern knowledge about the situations in which non-native (and native) speakers use their Englishes for real-life communication purposes, the sociocultural, cognitive and emotional processing conditions that bring about failure or success, and the strategies that speakers resort to when trying to cope with cultural and linguistic divergences and to reach certain communicative, self-expressive, or communal goals. Knowledge about these dimensions of ELF is the foundation on which the pupils can develop the kind of communicative language awareness and intercultural sensibility that leads to a deeper understanding and appreciation of the various manifestations of ELF. Implementation of these learning objectives in secondary school curricula needs to be informed by research input from grammatical and pragmatic descriptions of ELF (cf. House 2009; Mauranen 2009; Seidlhofer 2004, 2009; Seidlhofer et al. 2006), empirical investigations of strategic phenomena such as 'let it pass', monitoring, conversation management, or accommodation (cf. Firth 1996; House 1999, 2002; Jenkins 2000; Knapp & Meierkord 2002; Mauranen 2006, 2010) as well as analyses of non-native speaker attitudes and preferences on ELF (cf. Jenkins 2007).

A second range of learning objectives concerns the pupils' *ability to understand* other non-native speakers of English. In this connection, the Educational Standards for schools in the province of Baden-Württemberg make reference in particular to Indian English. This is in line with a more comprehensive, 'anglophone' understanding of English cultural and literary studies. Seen from a practical communication point of view, however, this extension does not really account for the immediate ELF challenges that pupils, and later students and professionals, are confronted with in the European context. Due to specific contrasts between the language pairs (L1/L2) involved and due to different levels of proficiency and different pedagogic approaches as well, communication between non-native speakers from different European countries can be quite challenging. First insights into these complex matters were provided by empirical studies carried out by Jennifer Jenkins (2000). On the basis of experimental evidence, she identified Standard English pronunciation features which need to be kept to ensure intelligibility and separated them as 'lingua franca core' from 'non-core' features that allow for non-native speaker variation, i.e., deviation from the standard norm, without loss of intelligibility. Contextual evidence does not always support these claims. For instance, according to Jenkins, the long/short vowel distinction belongs to the lingua franca core and should thus be respected. But Spanish speakers of English tend to pronounce, e.g., 'feel' with a short vowel as in 'fill' – usually, however, without any problems occurring even for less proficient listeners. Again, more extensive empirical investigations (cf. Ehrenreich 2009; Jenkins 2007) are required for linking ELF characteristics to intelligibility and comprehensibility and for preparing suitable pedagogic materials on this basis.

With regard to the pupils' own *production competence* and corresponding ELF-specific learning objectives, the situation is far less clear. Here, preferences and decisions concerning teaching and learning are particularly sensitive to the sociocultural and educational attitudes and values that are deemed important in the respective country, society or community. In German schools, for instance, the orientation towards British or American standard varieties is almost a constant (cf. Gnutzmann 2005). Related pedagogic prescriptions in curriculum specifications follow a societal consensus which is grounded in German and European political, sociocultural and educational development. From a more global perspective, however, it is obvious that this consensus is at odds with (semi-)official Englishes in other parts of the world and with current trends in ELF communication in Europe and elsewhere. To some extent, this is reflected in German school reality by a certain degree of relaxation that can be observed regarding Standard English norms: differences between what is laid down in curriculum regulations, what is actually taught, and what is learnt and accepted are quite noticeable.

However, the step from this kind of pedagogical 'let it pass' attitude to a principled and balanced decision is not a trivial one. Barbara Seidlhofer (2006: 45) convincingly argues that the pedagogic specification of teaching and learning objectives needs to be based on linguistic descriptions of ELF and, at the same time, should take account of the societal and pedagogic context in which these decisions are embedded. This position is in keeping with Widdowson's (1991) distinction between pedagogic prescription and linguistic description:

> The prescription of language for such contexts of instruction can, and should be, informed by the description of language in contexts of use, but not determined by it […] For prescription has its own conditions of adequacy to meet, and it is the business of language pedagogy, and nobody else's business, to propose what these conditions might be.   (p. 23)

The question is, what are pedagogically relevant conditions for deciding the direction in which a non-native speaker-learner should (be allowed to) develop his or her English?

Combining EFL and ELF

The social constructivist understanding of ELF makes it possible, and necessary, to also grant *learners* of English as a foreign language (EFL) the status of ELF *speakers* – provided they use their English for authentic communication purposes. In this constellation, Standard English rubs shoulders with ELF and it is necessary to further clarify the pedagogic relationship between the two. From the constructivist-developmental perspective sketched out above two complementary forces can be distinguished: the non-native speaker-learners' identification with themselves, and their identification with other (native or non-native) speakers of English.

In ELF research, identification with oneself goes hand in hand with an emancipatory stance and fits well with the *My English* condition. It is in this sense that Jenkins (2005) points to the dangers of an all too rigid pedagogic modelling of teaching and learning objectives on Standard English norms. With reference to pronunciation, she argues in favour of more freedom and greater flexibility: non-native speakers (learners) should be allowed to develop an accent that shows their cultural and linguistic roots; they should learn to identify and feel comfortable with their own variety of English.

But this is only half of the picture. A speaker-learner's identity is also strongly influenced and shaped by contact with other people, groups or cultures – which may involve native or non-native speaker communities or combinations of both. 'Contact', however, can take different forms. For a better understanding of a non-native speaker-learner's contact with a target language community, Knapp's (1987:1027) distinction between 'membership' and 'participation' is particularly helpful. While non-native speaker-learners are usually not members of their target speech communities, they may want to participate. In this connection, it should also be noted that the driving forces behind communal identity building reside in attitudes and values that form part of the speaker-learner's *construction* of otherness. The contact forces underlying construction, however, are not limited to direct and frequent interaction. For European ELF speakers with a learning background in EFL, it is perfectly natural to have most of their communicative contact with other non-native speakers and, at the same time, feel communally attracted to native speaker and Standard English characteristics and values.

Non-native speaker-learners' *My English* intuition may thus incorporate a diverse and heterogeneous range of requirements of performance and related linguistic competences; all strongly reflecting the speaker-learners' sociocultural and linguistic construction of native and non-native communities in relation to their own self. This is the 'primordial soup' in which *My English* is acquired and developed. A social constructivist perspective provides the theoretical foundation on which the fruitful interaction of seemingly conflicting and mutually exclusive forces can be understood. Against this backdrop, a speaker-learner's target orientation towards (native speaker) Standard English needs to be relativized in two ways. On the one hand, as we have seen, it is the result of the speaker-learner's perceptual and intentional construction and thus not the same as what linguists try to construct in the course of scientific linguistic description. On the other hand, a speaker-learner's target orientation is a shape-shifting target, continually transformed by social constructivist processes of acquisition and development.

From an applied linguistics perspective, these complex issues require descriptions that take into account a wide and diversified array of speaker variables: from communicative and communal needs and requirements to attitudes and preferences, from linguistic and communicative competences to products of performance and strategic processes, from state descriptions to longitudinal analyses of how linguistic and communicative competences and communal alliances change over time and are subject to involvement in particular ELF interactions. Such descriptions feed into (prescriptive) pedagogic decisions regarding a particular blend of ELF elements considered suitable for the German (and European) school context. As we saw above (Widdowson 1991:23), however, pedagogic prescription never follows directly from description. While respecting given sociocultural and educational framework conditions (which one might want to change as well, of course), pedagogic prescription rather exploits and mediates descriptive insights.

In light of our discussion, the challenge of pedagogic mediation is to bring EFL and ELF objectives into a certain balance that best serves the *My English* needs and requirements of the pupils. Sociolinguistic and pragmatic analyses have shown us ELF communication outside and beyond the foreign language classroom. The need for pedagogic interventions that help close the gap between school and real life has become obvious and urgent. Insights from the social constructivist perspective emphasize the natural inevitability for speaker-learners to develop their own English, thus backing up the general call for pedagogic change. The spaces that open up with the constructivist re-conceptualization of language learning become available now for pedagogically aligning the foreign language classroom with the communicative and communal needs and purposes of (future) speakers of English as a lingua franca.

Conclusion

As I hope to have shown, a social constructivist model of ELF and the acknowledgement of the *My English* condition enable a fresh look at the native speaker and Standard English issue that has preoccupied researchers and pedagogues from ELF and EFL contexts alike. Non-native ownership of English emerges as 'naturally' compatible with having a preference for Standard English, or for more 'real' versions of native speaker English or any other variety of English, including creoles and pidgins for that matter. On the basis of an understanding of second language acquisition as a complex process of cognitive, emotional and social construction, ownership of English is not a matter of choice but of biological-cognitive design: it is only by construction that people can develop and use their *own* English; and this includes choosing their own target language orientation by construction as well.

The argument in this article is primarily a theoretical and methodological one. It opens up new empirical perspectives for ELF and SLA research; and it has fruitful implications for ELF pedagogy and 'foreign' language teaching.

Acknowledgements

I would like to thank Barbara Seidlhofer for her detailed comments on an earlier version of this article. Her questions and arguments helped me clarify my own thinking. Any remaining misunderstandings are my own responsibility.

References

Albl-Mikasa, M. 2009. Who's afraid of ELF: "Failed" natives or non-native speakers struggling to express themselves? In *Dimensionen der Zweitsprachenforschung. Dimensions of Second Language Research*. (Festschrift for Kurt Kohn), M. Albl-Mikasa, S. Braun & S. Kalina, (eds), 109–129. Tübingen: Narr.
Byram, M. 1997. *Teaching and Assessing Intercultural Communicative Competence*. Clevedon: Multilingual Matters.

Canagarajah, S. 2007. Lingua franca English, multilingual communities, and language acquisition. *The Modern Language Journal* 91: 923–939.

Corder, S. P. 1967. The significance of learners' errors. *International Review of Applied Linguistics* 5: 161–170.

Council of Europe. 2001. *Common European Framework of References for Languages: Learning, Teaching, Assessment.* Cambridge: CUP.

Crystal, D. 2003. *English as a Global Language.* Cambridge: CUP.

Canale, M. & Swain, M. 1980. Theoretical bases of communicative approaches to second language teaching and testing. *Applied Linguistics* 1(1): 1–47.

Ehrenreich, S. 2009. English as a lingua franca in multinational corporations. Exploring business communities of practice. In *English as a Lingua Franca: Studies and Findings*, A. Mauranen & E. Ranta (eds), 126–151. Newcastle upon Tyne: Cambridge Scholars Publishing.

Færch, C. & Kasper, G. 1983. *Strategies in Interlanguage Communication.* London: Longman.

Firth, A. 1996. The discursive accomplishment of normality. On 'lingua franca' English and conversation analysis. *Journal of Pragmatics* 26: 237–259.

Gnutzmann, C. 2005. 'Standard English' and 'World English'. Linguistic and pedagogical considerations. In *The Globalisation of English and the English Classroom*, C. Gnutzmann & F. Intemann (eds), 107–118. Tübingen: Narr.

Graddol, D. 1997. *The Future of English? A Guide to Forecasting the Popularity of the English Language in the 21st Century.* London: British Council.

Graddol, D. 1999. The decline of the native speaker. *AILA Review* 13: 57–68.

Graddol, D. 2006. *English Next. Why Global English May Mean the End of 'English as a Foreign Language'.* London: British Council.

House, J. 1999. Misunderstanding in intercultural communication: Interactions in English as a lingua franca and the myth of mutual intelligibility. In *Teaching and Learning English as a Global Language – Native and Non-Native Perspectives*, C. Gnutzmann (ed.), 73–89. Tübingen: Stauffenburg.

House, J. 2002. Pragmatic competence in lingua franca English. In *Lingua Franca Communication*, K. Knapp & C. Meierkord (eds), 245–267. Frankfurt: Peter Lang.

House, J. 2009. Subjectivity in English as lingua franca discourse: The case of *you know. Intercultural Pragmatics* 6(2): 171–193.

James, A. 2005. The challenges of the lingua franca: English in the world and types of variety. In *The Globalisation of English and the English Classroom*, C. Gnutzmann & F. Intemann (eds), 133–144. Tübingen: Narr.

Jenkins, J. 2000. *The Phonology of English as an International Language.* Oxford: OUP.

Jenkins, J. 2005. Teaching pronunciation for English as a lingua franca. In *The Globalisation of English and the English Classroom*, C. Gnutzmann & F. Intemann (eds), 145–158. Tübingen: Narr.

Jenkins, J. 2006. Points of view and blind spots: ELF and SLA. *International Journal of Applied Linguistics* 16(2): 137–162.

Jenkins, J. 2007. *English as a Lingua Franca: Attitude and Identity.* Oxford: OUP.

Kachru, B. 1985. Standards, codification and sociolinguistic realism: The English in the outer circle. In *English in the World: Teaching and Learning the Language and Literatures*, R. Quirk & H. G. Widdowson (eds), 11–30. Cambridge: CUP.

Kachru, B. 1991. Liberation linguistics and the Quirk concern. *English Today* 7(1): 3–13.

Klimpfinger, T. 2009. 'She's mixing the two languages together' – Forms and functions of code-switching in English as a lingua franca. In *English as a Lingua Franca: Studies and Findings*, A. Mauranen & E. Ranta (eds), 348–371. Newcastle upon Tyne: Cambridge Scholars Publishing.

Knapp, K. 1987. English as an international lingua franca and the teaching of intercultural communication. In *Perspectives of Language in Performance. Studies in Linguistics, Literary Criticism, and Foreign Language Teaching to Honour Werner Hüllen on the Occasion of his Sixtieth Birthday*, W. Lörscher & R. Schulze (eds), 1022–1039. Tübingen: Narr.

Knapp, K. 2002. The fading out of the non-native speaker: Native dominance in lingua-franca-situations. In *Lingua Franca Communication*, K. Knapp & C. Meierkord (eds), 217–244. Frankfurt: Peter Lang.

Knapp, K. 2009. English as a lingua franca in Europe – variety, varieties or different types of use? In *Dimensionen der Zweitsprachenforschung. Dimensions of Second Language Research.* (Festschrift for Kurt Kohn), M. Albl-Mikasa, S. Braun & S. Kalina (eds), 131–139. Tübingen: Narr.

Knapp, K., Enninger, W. & Knapp-Potthoff, A. (eds). 1987. *Analyzing Intercultural Communication*. Berlin: Mouton-de Gruyter.

Knapp, K. & Meierkord, C. (eds). 2002. *Lingua Franca Communication*. Frankfurt: Peter Lang.

Kohn, K. 1990. *Dimensionen lernersprachlicher Performanz. Theoretische und empirische Untersuchungen zum Zweitsprachenerwerb*. Tübingen: Narr.

Kohn, K. 2007. Englisch als globale Lingua Franca: Eine Herausforderung für die Schule. In *Mehrsprachigkeit bei Kindern und Erwachsenen*, T. Anstatt (ed.), 207–222. Tübingen: Narr.

Landesbildungsserver. 2004. *Baden-Württemberg – Bildungsstandards für Englisch in Gymnasien*. <http://www.schule-bw.de/entwicklung/bistand> (May 29, 2010).

Leung, C. 2005. Convivial communication: Recontextualizing communicative competence. *International Journal of Applied Linguistics* 15(2): 119–144.

Mauranen, A. 2006. Signalling and preventing misunderstanding in English as lingua franca communication. *International Journal of the Sociology of Language* 177: 123–150.

Mauranen, A. 2009. Chunking in ELF: Expressions for managing interaction. *Journal of Intercultural Pragmatics* 6(2): 217–233.

Mauranen, A. 2010. Discourse reflexivity – a discourse universal? The case of ELF. *Nordic Journal of English Studies* 9 (2): 13–40.

Mauranen, A. & Ranta, E. (eds). 2009. *English as a Lingua Franca: Studies and Findings*. Newcastle upon Tyne: Cambridge Scholars Publishing.

Mauranen, A., Hynninen, N. & Ranta, E. 2010. English as an academic lingua franca: The ELFA project. *English for Specific Purposes* 29: 183–190.

Pitzl, M.-L. 2009. 'We should not wake up any dogs': Idiom and metaphor in ELF. In *English as a Lingua Franca: Studies and Findings*, A. Mauranen & E. Ranta (eds), 298–322. Newcastle upon Tyne: Cambridge Scholars Publishing.

Quirk, R. 1985. The English language in global context. In *English in the World: Teaching and Learning the Language and Literatures*, R. Quirk & H. G. Widdowson (eds), 1–6. Cambridge: CUP.

Quirk, R. 1990. Language varieties and standard language. *English Today* 21: 3–10.

Schumann, J. H. 1978. *The Pidginization Process. A Model for Second Language Acquisition*. Rowley MA: Newbury House.

Seidlhofer, B. 2001. Closing a conceptual gap: The case for a description of English as a lingua franca. *International Journal of Applied Linguistics* 11: 133–158.

Seidlhofer, B. 2004. Research perspectives on teaching English as a lingua franca. *Annual Review of Applied Linguistics* 24: 209–239.

Seidlhofer, B. 2005. Standard future or half-baked quackery? Descriptive and pedagogic bearings on the globalisation of English. In *The Globalisation of English and the English Classroom*, C. Gnutzmann & F. Intemann (eds), 159–173. Tübingen: Narr.

Seidlhofer, B. 2006. English as a lingua franca in the expanding circle: What it isn't. In *English in the World: Global Rules, Global Roles*, R. Rubdy & M. Saraceni (eds), 40–50. London: Continuum.

Seidlhofer, B. 2007. English as a lingua franca and communities of practice. In *Anglistentag 2006 Halle Proceedings*, S. Volk-Birke & J. Lippert (eds), 307–18. Trier: Wissenschaftlicher Verlag Trier.

Seidlhofer, B. 2009. Orientations in ELF research: Form and function. In *English as a Lingua Franca: Studies and Findings*, A. Mauranen & E. Ranta (eds), 37–59. Newcastle upon Tyne: Cambridge Scholars Publishing.

Seidlhofer, B., Breiteneder, A. & Pitzl, M.-L. 2006. English as a lingua franca in Europe. *Annual Review of Applied Linguistics* 26: 1–34.

Seidlhofer, B. & Widdowson, H. G. 2009. Conformity and creativity in ELF and learner English. In *Dimensionen der Zweitsprachenforschung. Dimensions of Second Language Research*, (Festschrift for Kurt Kohn), M. Albl-Mikasa, S. Braun & S. Kalina (eds), 93–107. Tübingen: Narr.

Selinker, L. 1972. Interlanguage. *International Review of Applied Linguistics* 10: 219–231.

Selinker, L. & Lamendella, J. T. 1980. Two perspectives on fossilization in interlanguage learning. In *Reading on English as a Second Language*, K. Croft (ed.), 132–143. Boston MA: Little, Brown and Company.

Swain, M. 1985. Communicative competence: Some roles of comprehensible input and comprehensible output in its development. In *Input in Second Language Acquisition*, S. Gass & C. Madden (eds), 235–256. New York NY: Newbury House.

Swain, M. 1995. Three functions of output in second language learning. In *Principle and Practice in Applied Linguistics. Studies in Honour of H. G. Widdowson*, G. Cook & B. Seidlhofer (eds), 125–144. Oxford: OUP.

Swain, M. 2005. The output hypothesis: Theory and research. In *Handbook of Research in Second Language Teaching and Learning*, E. Hinkel (ed.), 471–483. Mahwah NJ: Lawrence Erlbaum Associates.

Vygotsky, L. S. 1978. *Mind in Society: The Development of Higher Mental Processes*. Cambridge MA: Harvard University Press.

Wenger, E. 1998. *Communities of Practice*. Cambridge: CUP.

Widdowson, H. G. 1991. The description and prescription of language. In *Linguistics and Language Pedagogy: The State of the Art*, J. Alatis (ed.), 11–24. Washington DC: Georgetown University Press.

Widdowson, H. G. 2003. *Defining Issues in English Language Teaching*. Oxford: OUP.

Widdowson, H. G. 2004. *Text, Context, Pretext. Critical Issues in Discourse Analysis*. Oxford: Blackwell.

Corpora

ELFA (English as a Lingua Franca in Academic Settings): <http://www.eng.helsinki.fi/elfa/> (May 29, 2010).

TELF (Tübingen English as a Lingua Franca): <http://www.telf.uni-tuebingen.de/> (May 29, 2010).

VOICE (Vienna Oxford International Corpus of English): <http://www.univie.ac.at/voice/> (May 29, 2010).

The early acquisition of English as a second language

The case of young Chinese learners of English in Britain

Li Wei

Birkbeck College, University of London, UK

One aspect of English in Europe today, particularly in Britain, is the fact that many children with an L1 that is not English acquire English outside the home at a very early age. This paper focuses on the acquisition of English by young Chinese children who were born in China but moved to Britain at around one year of age. As such this paper addresses the underexplored area of early acquisition of a second language prior to age three. The analyses focus on lexical acquisition, the use of code-switching and early grammatical learning of English. The results are discussed in relation to a number of hotly debated issues in the literature on bilingual first and early second language acquisition.

Introduction

One prominent feature of English in Europe today is the increasing number of children with an L1 that is not English who acquire English outside the home at a very early age (i.e. before the age of three), when their L1 is not yet fully developed. This is particularly the case in Britain, with large numbers of children born to parents who are not English L1 speakers and who are exposed to languages other than English at home. Whilst official statistics are hard to obtain, media reports have led us to believe that one in three of the children in London's schools, for example, speak languages other than English at home.

There has been a variety of studies of the so-called EAL (English as an additional language) children in Europe, their language use, school achievements and identity development (e.g. Extra & Yağmur 2004; Cenoz & Jessner 2000; Leung 2001). In this article, we focus on the acquisition of English by young Chinese children who were born in China but moved to Britain at around one year of age. They continue to be exposed to Chinese L1 from their parents at home, and begin to learn English from other sources of input. They are acquiring English as a second language. They are part of a global population movement which, although by no means new, has increased significantly in the last twenty years. Europe and North America have been on the receiving end of this movement. The latest report from the UK government's Department of Education (13 May 2010) suggests that 25.5% primary school pupils are classified as non-white British in 2010 and 905,610 children do not speak English as a first language, a rise of 42,750 in 12 months.

Research on early second language acquisition or ESLA has gone through an interesting path, In the 1970s a number of case studies of young L2 learners appeared. Amongst the ones whose subjects are of similar background and age to those in the present study are Burling's (1959) study of an English L1 child who began to hear a new language, Garo, at the age of 1;4, and Itoh and Hatch's (1978) study of a Japanese child with input in English through playschool starting at age 2;7. Fantini (1985) provided a case study of a Spanish L1 child who had regular exposure to English from the age of 2. These studies aimed to document the developmental paths of young L2 learners and to find out universal patterns. However, with the introduction of the Chomskian generative linguistics framework in the 1980s, research on second language acquisition (SLA) focused mostly on adult L2 learners. Since the 1990s, there has been some growth in studies of what some people call child SLA. Lakshmanan (2009) provides a survey of the recent studies of child SLA which tend to follow the Chomskyian framework of principles and parameters and focus on the mental representation of L2 grammars. In her summary of studies of ESLA, Tabors (2008) notes four developmental stages: (1) home language use, (2) the silent period, (3) formulaic L2 use, and (4) productive L2. Our discussion in this chapter is framed within a number of theoretical and methodological issues concerning early acquisition of a second language, but not from a generative perspective. I am particularly interested in the features of ESLA that seem to differ from those of adult SLA or from Bilingual First Language Acquisition (BFLA; see below).

The chapter is structured as follows: An outline of the differences between early second language acquisition, the focus of the present study, and other types of acquisition that involve a second or additional language is followed by a brief review of existing studies of young Chinese learners of English. The main body of the article is devoted to the study of three young Chinese children's acquisition of English after they arrived in England at the age of 1;2 to 1;7. A number of observations are made. On the basis of the observations and analyses, we propose two theoretical hypotheses for future research, which we discuss in the concluding section.

BFLA/BAMFLA, SLA and ESLA

Considerable progress has been made in the field of bilingual first language acquisition (BFLA), i.e., the simultaneous acquisition of two languages from birth, and bilingual and multilingual first language acquisition (BAMFLA), BFLA plus multilingual first language acquisition (see De Houwer 2009 for an up-to-date and comprehensive review of BFLA). In addition to the general theoretical issues of language acquisition such as input, context, interface of linguistic and other cognitive systems, BFLA and BAMFLA have raised a number of issues such as dominance, transfer, and cross-linguistic influence that seem to be particularly relevant to young bilingual and multilingual children. Some of these issues also concern early second language acquisition, or ESLA. The main distinction between ESLA and BFLA/BAMFLA is that there is a clear difference in the onset of exposure to the two languages in ESLA, whereas in BFLA or BAMFLA there is none. The difference can be between 12 and 36 months (McLaughlin 1978), although these cut-off points are somewhat arbitrary. The crucial fact is that when an ESLA child is exposed to L2 and begins to learn L2, his or her L1 is still developing and by no means stable. In some cases, when, for instance, the onset of exposure to L2 is at around 12 months of age, the child may not be able to produce much in L1 yet. Nevertheless, the child has had a consistent, monolingual input for an extended period of time. What impact this initial exposure to one language has on the acquisition of the later-exposed-to language is an important question to address in ESLA.

ESLA is clearly linked with second language acquisition (SLA) in general. Yet, SLA research usually concerns itself with much older learners, and the L2 input tends to be more distant from the learner's immediate social network, i.e., family and neighbourhood (see Doughty & Long 2003). The L1 in SLA is more firmly established than in ESLA; in fact, the L1 is usually fully developed. The learner in SLA is generally more aware of the differences between L1 and L2. Although researchers often opt for the more positive-sounding terminology of 'influence', their main concern is how the knowledge of L1 'interferes' with the acquisition process of and the ultimate attainment in L2. SLA research therefore investigates the various factors – linguistic, psychological, neurological, socio-cultural and pedagogical – that affect the acquisition of L2 from the initial state to what is referred to as ultimate achievement.

Whilst under-explored, ESLA raises important questions that are hotly debated in the existing literature on BFLA/BAMFLA as well as on SLA, such as dominance and transfer, cross-linguistic influence, input and context, the interface of linguistic and other cognitive systems, and the interface of different domains of language (e.g. phonology-lexicon; syntax-pragmatics). There are also issues that may well be unique to ESLA that should be investigated; for instance, what impact does the incoming L2 have on an L1 that is not yet stable? How does the child deal with structures that are not fully acquired in the L1 and that are significantly different in the L2? Would instances of codeswitching and translation be more frequent in this group of children than in BFLA or BAMFLA? What impact does the drastic change in social environment which usually accompanies ESLA have on language development? While the present study cannot address all these issues in depth, we will present data which may help to develop theoretical and methodological questions for future research.

Young Chinese learners of English

There has been considerable growth in the study of Chinese children who are also acquiring languages other than Chinese. Yip and Matthews (2007) present a detailed documentation of their corpus-based study of six children with a one-parent-one-language background who are acquiring Cantonese and English simultaneously from birth. Focussing on their own three children, Yip and Matthews test a number of theoretical concepts and hypotheses concerning BFLA, especially transfer and vulnerable domains, as well as more general issues such as contact induced linguistic change, i.e., grammaticalization. Studies in Li Wei's (2010) collection follow a similar line of enquiry and examine the acquisition of certain grammatical features, pronouns as well as phonology by Chinese children in bilingual and trilingual contexts (Chan 2010; Gu 2010; Chang-Smith 2010; Qi 2010; Yang & Zhu 2010).

A number of studies exist concerning Chinese children's acquisition of English as a second language at a young age. Most of them, however, focus on school-aged children who are receiving immersion education in English speaking schools in English-speaking countries or who are attending intensive English classes in China (e.g. Xiao 2002). Jia and Aaronson (2003), for example, carried out a longitudinal study of ten Chinese children who emigrated to the United States of America between ages 5 and 16 over a three year period, and examined the changes in their language preferences, language environments and proficiency in English as L2 and in L1 Chinese. On the basis of L2 English grammaticality judgement tests, L1 Chinese to L2 English translation, and parental ratings, Jia and Aaronson argue that age of arrival, previous education level, and language environment including reading environment and speaking and listening environments are crucial factors in learning outcomes of English as well as the maintenance of L1.

A group of studies that focus on much younger Chinese children learning English are those of adoptees from China. For obvious reasons, these children's

Chinese L1 development is not systematically documented. Once they have been adopted into English-speaking families, it is rarely possible for them to continue with sustained input in Chinese. Nicoladis & Grabois (2002) reported on a case of rapid acquisition of English and loss of Chinese by a child adopted from China into a Canadian family. Similarly, Pollock, Price & Fulmer (2003), Krakow & Roberts (2003), Roberts, Krakow & Pollock (2003) reported on a series of studies of Chinese adoptees in American families, all of which point to the fact that the majority of the children can develop English very fast and with little difficulty. The researchers suggested that it was the supportive language environment provided by the receiving families that facilitated this apparent rapid progress. It would be interesting to ask if the fact that the children did have a L1, however incomplete its development may have been, had a facilitating effect. In some sense, these children are acquiring a 'second first language', rather than a second language in the conventional sense.

The study presented in this chapter is different from the ones mentioned so far. It is about children who have moved from a monolingual Chinese environment to an English-dominant bilingual environment at a very young age. Their L1 Chinese is not fully developed. It continues to develop while the children are acquiring English as L2. The L2 input is much greater in variety than that in L1. The study represents an extension of our earlier work on the development of L1 (Chinese) in an L2 (English) dominant environment (Li Wei & Lee 2002). The focus of the present study is on the development of English as L2.

The sample

We have followed three young children, two girls and one boy, who moved to Britain from China with their parents after one year of age. The parents are native Mandarin speakers and continue to speak Mandarin with each other and with the children at home. All the parents also speak English to various degrees. Initial input of English came from television and interactions with neighbours and in service encounters (e.g. shopping, going to the doctor). The researchers got to know the parents and the children as soon as they arrived in Britain and visited the families regularly. Formal observation and data collection started after a minimum of six months.

The number of Chinese words consists of types and were reported by the parents through language diaries that they were asked to keep prior to the visit.

It was decided that monthly observations and recordings would be made once the children reached the 50-word stage in Mandarin, although some recordings and tests (e.g. picture naming) were done earlier for a separate purpose

Table 1. Background information of the sample

Name	Gender	Age of arrival in UK (year;month)	Age and number of Chinese words produced at 1st research visit	Parental English
Jade	Female	1;2	1;8–26	Father: advanced Mother: beginner
Neena	Female	1;7	2;0–70	Father: advanced Mother: intermediate
William	Male	1;4	2;0–52	Father: advanced Mother: intermediate

(phonology). The attainment of the 50-word stage is traditionally used by speech and language therapists to determine whether there is a developmental delay. It is also believed to be a first threshold for the development of syntax. In the case of Jade, the 50-word stage was reached when she was 1;11. The other two children reached the 50-word stage at around age 2;0. The data collection sessions lasted between one and two hours each time and consisted of the following:

1. interviews with the parents about the children's general development, any significant changes in the environment that might affect the children's language development, parental language use, and new words and phrases they had heard the children produce;
2. recorded conversations with the children during play with the parents and/or the researcher;
3. picture naming during the first three visits, using the pictures for the phonology test (Zhu Hua 2002);
4. story reading by parents and talking about the stories;
5. later in the data collection process, children's telling of stories over picture books.

All the recordings were made at the children's family homes. During the initial visits, most of the interactions were in Mandarin and the researcher spoke mostly Mandarin to the children. As the children began to be exposed to English, both Mandarin and English were used during the research visits. The data were transcribed by the researcher, which were later checked and verified by a second Mandarin-English bilingual researcher who has experience in child language research.

In order to analyse the children's lexical development, the recorded language samples where processed according to a CDI-style word list and a LARSP-style language profile chart (published in Li Wei & Zhu Hua 2003). The Chinese word

Table 2. Early English word production and first regular English exposure

Child	Age of starting English daycare/ nursery (year;month)	Regular, spontaneous English production (number of word types)
Jade	2;6	18
Neena	2;9	30
William	2;5	11

list was modelled on the Bates-MacArthur Communicative Development Inventory (Fenson, Dale, Reznick, Thal, Bates, Hartung, Pethick & Reilly 1993), but is not a Chinese translation of it. It was used in some earlier studies (e.g. Zhu Hua & Li Wei 1999). Similarly, the language profile chart is based on the Language Assessment, Remediation and Screening Procedure (LARSP), originally developed in English by Crystal, Fletcher & Garman (1976), but ours takes into consideration the unique structural features of the Chinese language.

In England, state-funded nursery education is available from the age of 3, and may be full-time or part-time. If registered with a state school, children can be enrolled in the reception year in September of the school year, thus beginning school at age 4 or 4;6. Attendance is compulsory beginning with the term following the child's fifth birthday. As the parents of the children in our sample are all professionals or research students, they were eager to send the children to nursery at the first possible date so that they could have more time for their work or studies. Two of the children, Jade and William, attended private day-care for 3 or 4 hours before they started nursery school, Jade started at the age of 2;6 and William at the age of 2;5. Neena did not attend private daycare but managed to get into nursery school at the age of 2;9. All the day care centres and nurseries were English speaking. There was no other Chinese speaker at any of them.

Table 2 gives information on the children's English language production when they began to attend day care and nursery.

As indicated before, monthly data collection continued in both Chinese and English until the children reached 500 words in English. The timing was determined by using the word list in the Bates-MacArthur CDI (Fenson et al. 1993), which was recorded and checked by both the researcher and the parents. The parents were issued copies of the CDI and asked to keep records. The researcher also made notes during the observations and used the checklist to process the data from the recordings. As the children began to speak English, the parents also spoke some English with them. However, they spoke primarily Chinese at home. Observation and recording continued less regularly (at two or three months intervals) for one further year afterwards, focusing on the children's English language development.

Before looking at the data in detail, I want to outline the social network contacts of the three children during the periods we studied them.

Social networks and family visits

In various previous studies of bilingual children, we considered the effect of social network contacts on their language development (e.g. Li Wei 1993; Raschka, Li Wei & Lee 2002). In the present study, we examined this effect on the children's early second language acquisition and on their use of the two languages. Initially, the children spent most of their time with their parents. The amount of time they spent together in joint activities such as reading, playing games and having dinner was considerable. Most of the joint activities were conducted in Mandarin Chinese, with translations to English of specific words that the parents wanted the children to learn. Gradually, the children had more contacts with neighbours and other English speakers. Although the contacts were of a general social kind, the children had more opportunities to communicate in English only. They also learned different ways of greeting people and politeness routines. For example, we observed Neena saying "Raining" to a neighbour after she greeted her. The neighbour responded by saying "That's right. It's raining, isn't it? What a clever girl". Stylistic and addressee-oriented variations in language use are an integral part of the children's pragmatic competence. Once they started attending day care centres and nurseries, they then had a specific setting in which English is used. This enabled them to produce unilingual utterances in English (see also De Houwer 2005). Indeed, the children very quickly learned to separate the two languages according to the context and they knew that only English was expected at the day care centre or nursery. They rarely used Chinese words there, although they continued to use both Chinese and English at home.

During our observation with the children, two of the families had short visits from the children's grandparents and other relatives. All three families paid home visits to China. These periods of intensive contacts with Chinese-only speakers clearly helped the children's Mandarin as they learned many new words and phrases and had more opportunities to communicate in Chinese only. Nevertheless, there is no evidence to suggest that these visits had any negative impact on the children's learning of English. They all seemed to have maintained what they had learned very well and continued to acquire new words and structures while in China. What these short family visits did effect was to raise the children's awareness of the separate contextual requirements for the two languages. They had a much better understanding of which language to use to whom and when.

In the following sections, I focus on some aspects of the children's development of English as a second language and relate some of this development to that of the L1, Chinese.

Observations

Early appearances of English

For all three children, English words appeared spontaneously in their production almost as soon as they arrived in Britain. They realised immediately that they were now living in an English speaking environment, and began saying some English words to people they met as well as to their parents at home. Most of the words were formulaic, social words. The top ten most frequently occurring English words were *no, hello, bye bye, thank you, sorry, yes, TV, cheese, car* and *good*.

The parents confirmed that the children knew these words before they left China. The parents had quite explicitly taught some of the words to the children. They children had also been taught other English words in China, mostly nouns such as *apple, water, sun, tree, bike* and occasionally others like *go, in, out*. The word "cheese" may seem strange in the top ten list. However, it is commonly used by Chinese people to prompt a smile when they are having a photograph taken. Neena was seen to use this word when she was pretending to hold a toast. It was probably because she heard the parents saying *cheers* in a Chinese accent which sounded very much like *cheese*.

Amongst the first English words that we are certain that were learned after the children arrived in Britain were *mommy* and *wee wee*. They also gradually replaced *TV* with *telly*, which is most commonly heard in England. Animal names also began to appear more frequently, e.g. *dog, cat, sheep, horse,* as the children's encounters with animals increased in England.

The first instances of mixing were all English words embedded in a Chinese utterance. Again, most of the embedded English words were formulaic, social words and took the form of islands. Increasingly, the children started mixing English words which had culturally specific referents, such as *bread, ham, curry, spaghetti* (or *ghetti* as most children say).

The spontaneous production of two-word utterances with a predicate occurred at different times for the three children. These were utterances like *go out,* and did not include multi-word noun phrases such as *apple juice*. Table 3 lists a few examples and shows both the number of words the children produced at the time when they were saying the two-word utterances and their biological age.

Table 3. Appearance of two-word utterances in English

Child	Number of word types produced in English	Biological age (year;month)	Examples of two word utterances
Jade	29	2;9	*mommy eat; wash hand; go bed*
Neena	46	2;10	*watch telly; go out*
William	50	2;9	*have bath; sit down; ball play*

Translation equivalents

Consistent with findings from BFLA studies, translation equivalents appeared early in the children's spontaneous English production. The translation equivalents were determined by checking all the English words that the children produced with our recordings of their Chinese words. All three children had instances of translation equivalents in the first 30 English words. Some of the initial translation equivalents were taught specifically by the parents and referred to common household objects or things in everyday life, e.g. *table, light, window, glass, water, fish, dog*.

The total number of words thresholds at the bottom of Figure 1 (50 to 300) are cumulative English word types as measured by the CDI. The percentages refer to the ratio of English words that had translation equivalents in the children's Chinese production against the total of their English words produced at the time. So 60% at 50 words point would mean approximately 30 out of the 50 had Chinese equivalents already.

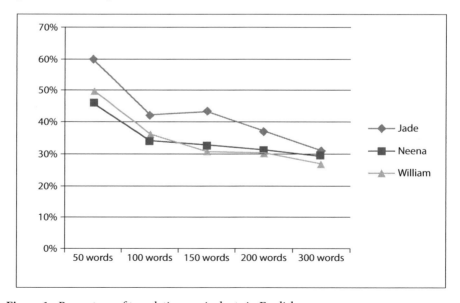

Figure 1. Percentage of translation equivalents in English

Table 4. Number of one-to-many equivalents out of total translation equivalents (in brackets) at 300-word (English) stage

Jade	Neena	William
16 (93)	12 (88)	11 (80)

As we can see from Figure 1, the percentage of translation equivalents was higher during the initial stages of English L2 acquisition. This may be due to the fact that the children were relearning the names for the same objects in English. All the translation equivalents before the 150-word stage were open class, content words.

More complex translation equivalents began to appear at around the 200-word stage in the children's English L2 development. We observed some very interesting features. For example, Chinese has a verb, *bao*, meaning *cuddle* and *carry* usually at the front rather than on the back. Initially, all children continued to use the Chinese word for this action, often in a request to be carried up or down stairs, for instance, even if they were attempting to speak English. Later, they started to differentiate the two component meanings and produced two English verbs, *cuddle* and *carry*. Cases like these represent a methodological challenge in terms of calculating the number of translation equivalents (see also De Houwer, Bornstein & De Coster 2006). In the present study we calculated both English verbs as one translation equivalent in order to get the baseline figures for the overall number of translation equivalents. There is also the question of what triggers translation equivalents. Semantic or conceptual compatibility seems to be a factor in the examples we have observed. There are two broad types of translation equivalents: one-to-one exact or near-exact match in terms of semantics, usually object names; and one-to-many component equivalents, such as *bao* to *cuddle* and *carry*. There is a marked increased in the second type, one-to-many, translation equivalents at later stages of L2 acquisition.

The appearance of translation equivalents implies that some of the interactions between the children and their parents were in English. The parents did report that they occasionally code-switched between Chinese and English. The children were certainly aware that if they said anything in English, the parents could understand them equally well when they spoke Chinese.

Time lag between the two languages in terms of vocabulary size
Before we discuss other aspects of the children's L2 English, it is useful to consider the differences in the development of L1 and L2. Table 5 gives the English vocabulary size of the children against the milestones for Chinese vocabulary established by the Chinese word list.

Table 5. Vocabulary development in English in spontaneous production

Chinese vocabulary	Jade	Neena	William
50	4	–	3
100	10	14	9
150	42	50	35
200	70	85	66
300	126	140	103
400	246	287	235
500	332	350	302

Neena reached the 50-word stage in Chinese before we started recording her. On the whole the children started slowly in English and with a considerable gap between the two languages. But the difference became much closer towards the end of our structured observation.

Mean length of utterance

It is difficult to present a meaningful comparison of mean length of utterance in the two languages, as notion of a Chinese word can mean either a single syllable-character or a disyllabic double character unit. The latter is a more common semantic unit in contemporary spoken Chinese. But structurally, such units are usually made up of two components, each of which may stand alone for different syntactic functions. For instance, *chi-fan* (eat) consists of *chi* (eat) and *fan* (meal), which would make a verb-object phrase. But in spoken Chinese *chi-fan* is often used as one unified semantic unit and as a single verb. How to count such units depends on the analyst's theoretical assumptions. The acquisition of Chinese disyllabic words with various syntactic relations is a highly interesting topic. But straightforward comparisons with morpheme counting in English are impossible if at all meaningful.

Transfer from Mandarin to English

Chinese remained the dominant language throughout the study period, although there was a clear context differential after the children had started attending English playgroup and nursery school. We observed a number of examples of syntactic transfer from Chinese to English, but rarely vice versa. This is probably because most of the Chinese speakers they interacted with also knew English, whereas no Chinese speaker was available in the English speaking context, i.e., the nursery school. English words did often occur in Chinese utterances, but in most cases they were instances of code-mixing or code-switching. Of the Chinese to English transfers, the most common examples were those of one-to-many translation equivalents where the child would over-generalize and use only one of the translation equivalents for all functions. For instance, the Chinese word *shang* can be a position word, meaning *up* or *upward*, as well as a verb, meaning *go up, mount, board* or *get on*. All three children have produced, on different occasions, utterances such as "up bed", meaning *go to bed*, "up stairs", meaning *go upstairs*, "up car", meaning *get into the car*. These seem to be direct translations from Chinese *shang chuang, shang louti* and *shang che*, where *shang* is translated into the wrong lexical category.

In Yip and Matthew's (2007) study of Bilingual First Language Acquisition, examples of Cantonese to English transfer are specifically related to verb-particle constructions.

> *she wake up me* (Sophie 2:05;16)
> *put in this* (Alice 2:00:26)   (Yip and Matthews 2007: 219)

Yip and Matthews argue that these child utterances are influenced by Cantonese structures such as *keoi giu seng nego*, literally *she call awake me*.

However, we do not have any examples of such production in our children. Instead, our children either omit the particle or the pronoun and produce utterances such as "she wake me" and "put in".

This brings us to a closely related issue, namely error patterns in the children's English production.

Error patterns
Many of the errors produced by our children resembled those of older Chinese learners of English as a second or foreign language, supporting the argument that BFLA and ESLA should be carefully differentiated in any study. They are of two broad types. One is wrong collocation. The other type is the omission of articles and prepositions.

Collocation errors are related to translation equivalents. The children in our study seemed to have problems when a Chinese word has several different translations whose usage depends on the context and intended meaning. For example, the Chinese verb *chuan* can be translated as *wear* or *put on* depending on the situation. Our children have been heard to say "wear shoe" when they meant *put on shoes*. Similarly, they have been recorded to say "open light" when they meant *switch on the light*. Such errors seem rare in L1 English.

English articles present a challenge to many learners. Our children routinely omited articles, as they did plural and third person singular marking. They also seemed to have a habit of omitting prepositions in verb phrases. For example, they would say "look picture" (omitting *at the*) and "listen song" (omitting *to a*).

Another common error was the confusion of words whose semantic differences are subtler and dependent on usage. For example, the children seemed to be unsure of the difference between *watch, see* and *look*, and produced utterances such as "watch film" (omitting *a*), "see film" (omitting *a*) and "look film" (omitting *at a*).

They also seemed to have problems with *look at a book* as opposed to *read a book*, probably because in Chinese *kan shu* can mean both.

Parental discourse style

We now move onto the possible effect of environmental factors on the children's early second language acquisition. In line with other existing studies of young bilingual children's language development (e.g., Lanza 2001), our data show a clear link between the parental discourse style and the children's acquisition of English as L2. By parental discourse style we mean the way they interact with the children, and not the way they interact between themselves. In theory, the way adults talk amongst themselves in front of the children should have an effect on the children's language acquisition as well. But it was not possible for us in the present study to collect sufficiently comprehensive and reliable data to ascertain the parents' discourse patterns. As in other studies we have undertaken, our focus here is on the joint activities the parents conduct with the children.

In a group study of French-English bilingual children, David and Li Wei (2008) found that some parents encouraged translation equivalents by prompting them to respond to the same questions in both languages. As a result, these children had significantly more translation equivalents than other children whose parents did not use this style. Our present study reveals similar findings, although the differences are in the same children over time rather than between the children. As Figure 1 shows earlier, the percentage of translation equivalents in the first 50 English words of the children was much higher than in the later stages of their L2 development. A significant part of this can be attributed to the fact that all the parents of the three children in our study explicitly taught the children translation equivalents and prompted them to produce translation equivalents in conversational interaction so the parents are in fact also a model for English! Translation was thus a common strategy in the early stages of second language acquisition generally for both the learners and the parent/teacher. But the discourse style of the parents in our sample also seems to have had an effect on the number of translation equivalents the children produced. Two examples are given below:

Extract (1)

Mother: *Zhishi shengme?* (Pointing to a picture in a picture book)

Jade: *Yaya* (= Duck)

Mother: *Yaya, zhen congming. Yingyu ne? Yingyu zhidao bu zhidao?*

    (= Duck. Really clever. In English? Do you know (what's it called in) English?)

Jade: *Duck.*

Mother: *Duck. Duila. Zhen congming a.*

    (Correct. Really clever.)

Extract (2)

William: *Doodooooo.* (Pretending to be a driver.)

Father: *Doodooooo. Kaiche a? kaide shenme che?*

    (Driving? What vehicle are you driving?)

William: *Doodooooo.*

Father: *Qiche haishi huoche?* (Car or train?)

William: *Doodooooo.*

Father: *Qiche haishi huoche?* (Car or train?)

William: *Huoche.* (Train.)

Father: *Is it train?*

William: *Doodoooo. Train, train.*

Clearly the effect of parental discourse style on translation equivalents can only be ascertained by more systematic studies with larger samples.

Summary and conclusion

This articles has presented a case study of three young Chinese children who came to Britain after the age of 1;0 and who have acquired English as a second language. Their Chinese L1 continued to grow while gradually they were developing their L2, English. The exposure of English started in a limited way, but gradually expanded both in quantity and variety through different social networks contacts. In the early stages of their L2 development, the children produced a higher proportion of translation equivalents. This was both a result of a parental discourse strategy which specifically prompted translation equivalents and of a general social need to learn the names of common objects in everyday life. Early syntactic development showed some influence of L1, where production errors can be attributed to transfer from L1 to L2. These instances of transfer were often related to one-to-many translation equivalents, where the child was in the process of learning the semantic properties of certain lexical items as well as the lexical categories and syntactic functions of words.

On the basis of the observations we made in the present study, we can propose two theoretical hypotheses for future research. First, with regard to translation equivalents and syntactic transfer, we propose the *Comparability Hypothesis* – items and structures that are conceptually, in semantic and syntactic terms, completely compatible or completely contrastive are acquired easily, whereas items and structures that are conceptually ambiguous in cross-linguistic comparison, e.g. that belong to different lexical categories in different languages, or that have additional semantic properties, may trigger more errors, transfers or translations.

Second, the *Input Style Hypothesis*. Both the quantity and variety of input have a direct impact on the number (quantity) and type (variety) of words and structures the children learn to produce in spontaneous conversation. We have seen specific examples of how the way parents talk to children may affect the children's use of translation equivalents. We also have examples of how the children learn to associate specific interactional styles with specific addressees. Future research can demonstrate the impact in quantitative terms through group comparisons and longitudinal studies.

Finally, the dynamic relationship between the two languages is an issue inviting further attention. The present study focuses on the development of L2 English. However, a key point in early second language acquisition is that the L1 continues to develop. What impact the incoming L2 has on the developing L1 and vice versa is something we have not addressed here, but a topic that needs to be taken seriously in future studies of ESLA.

In today's globalizing world, early second language acquisition is a commonplace phenomenon. It has an immediate relevance to thousands of children and their families worldwide. It also raises important theoretical and methodological questions for developing linguistics. It is hoped that the case study we present in this paper serves as a catalyst for more extensive research in this field.

Acknowledgements

I am grateful to the editors of this volume for their encouragement and understanding during the process of writing this paper. I am particularly grateful for the most constructive comments by Annick De Houwer.

References

Burling, R. 1959. Language development of a Garo and English-speaking child. *Word* 15: 45–68 (Reprinted in *Second Language Acquisition. A Book of Readings*, E. Hatch (ed.), 1978, 55–75, Rowley MA: Newbury House).

Cenoz, J. & Jessner, U. (eds). 2000. *English in Europe: The Acquisition of a Third Language*. Clevedon: Multilingual Matters.

Chan, A. 2010. The Cantonese double object construction with *bei2* 'give' in bilingual children. In *BAMFLA (Bilingual and Multilingual First Language Acquisition) of Chinese children*, Li Wei (ed.), A special issue of the *International Journal of Bilingualism* 14: 65–85.

Chang-Smith, M. 2010. Developmental pathways for first language acquisition of Mandarin nominal expressions: Comparing monolingual with simultaneous Mandarin–English bilingual children. In *BAMFLA (Bilingual and Multilingual First Language Acquisition) of Chinese children*, Li Wei (ed.), A special issue of the *International Journal of Bilingualism* 14: 11–35.

Crystal, D., Fletcher, P. & Garman, M. 1976. *The Grammatical Analysis of Language Disability*. London: Arnold.

David, A. & Li Wei. 2008. Individual differences in the lexical development of French-Englsh bilingual children. *International Journal of Bilingual Education and Bilingualism* 11: 598–618.

De Houwer, A. 2005. Early bilingual acquisition: Focus on morphosyntax and the Separate Development Hypothesis. In *The Handbook of Bilingualism*, J. Kroll & A. de Groot (eds), 30–48. Oxford: OUP.

De Houwer, A. 2009. *Bilingual First Language Acquisition*. Bristol: Multilingual Matters.

De Houwer, A., Bornstein, M. H. & De Coster, S. 2006. Early understanding of two words for the same thing: A CDI study of lexical comprehension in infant bilinguals. *International Journal of Bilingualism* 10: 331–347.

Doughty, C. & Long, M. 2003. *The handbook of Second Language Acquisition*. Oxford: Blackwell.

Extra, G. & Yağmur, K. (eds). 2004. *Urban Multilingualism in Europe: Immigrant Minority Languages at Home and School*. Clevedon: Multilingual Matters.

Fantini, A. 1985. *Language Acquisition of a Bilingual Child: A Sociolinguistic Perspective (to age ten)*. Clevedon: Multilingual Matters.

Fenson, L., Dale, P., Reznick, S., Thal, D., Bates, E., Hartung, J., Pethick, S. & Reilly, J. 1993. *MacArthur Communicative Development Inventories: User's Guide and Technical Manual*. San Diego CA: Singular Publishing Group.

Gu, C. C. 2010. Crosslinguistic influence in two directions: The acquisition of dative constructions in Cantonese-English bilingual children. In *BAMFLA (Bilingual and Multilingual First Language Acquisition) of Chinese children*, Li Wei (ed.), A special issue of the *International Journal of Bilingualism* 14: 87–103.

Itoh, H. & Hatch, E. 1978. Second Language Acquisition: A case study. In *Second Language Acquisition. A Book of Readings*, E. Hatch (ed.), 77–88. Rowley MA: Newbury House.

Jia, G. & Aaronson, D. 2003. A longitudinal study of Chinese children and adolescents learning English in the United States. *Applied Psycholinguistics* 24: 131–161.

Krakow, R. A. & Roberts, J. 2003. Acquisition of English vocabulary by young Chinese adoptees. *Journal of Multilingual Communication Disorders* 1: 169–176.

Lakshmanan, U. 2009. Child second language acquisition. In *The New Handbook of Second Language Acquisition*, W. Ritchie & T. Bhatia (eds), 377–399. Bingley: Emerald.

Lanza, E. 2001. Bilingual first language acquisition: A discourse perspective on language contact in parent–child interaction. In *Trends in Bilingual Acquisition*, J. Cenoz & F. Genesee (eds), 201–229. Amsterdam: John Benjamins.

Leung, C. 2001. English as an additional language: Distinct language focus or diffused curriculum concerns? *Language and Education* 15: 33–55.

Li Wei. 1993. Mother tongue maintenance in a Chinese community school in Newcastle upon Tyne: Developing a social network perspective. *Language and Education* 7: 199–215.

Li Wei. 2010. *BAMFLA (Bilingual and Multilingual First Language Acquisition) of Chinese children*. A special issue of the *International Journal of Bilingualism* 14: 3–9.

Li Wei & Lee, S. 2002. L1 development in an L2 environment: The use of Cantonese classifiers and quantifiers by young British-born Chinese in Tyneside. *International Journal of Bilingual Education and Bilingualism* 4: 359–382.

Li Wei & Zhu Hua. 2003. *Zenyang Peiyang Tiancai Ertong* (How to cultivate talented children) (in Chinese). Beijing: International Culture Publishing Company.

McLaughlin, B. 1978. *Second Language Acquisition in Childhood*, Vol. 1: *Preschool children*. Hillsdale NJ: Lawrence Erlbaum Associates.

Nicoladis, E. & Grabois, H. 2002. Learning English and losing Chinese: A case study of a child adopted from China. *International Journal of Bilingualism* 6: 441–454.

Pollock, K. E., Price, J. R. & Fulmer, K. C. 2003. Speech-language acquisition in children adopted from China: A longitudinal investigation of two children. *Journal of Multilingual Communication Disorders* 1: 184–193.

Qi, R. 2010. Pronoun acquisition in a Mandarin-English bilingual child. In *BAMFLA (Bilingual and Multilingual First Language Acquisition) of Chinese children*, Li Wei (ed.), A special issue of the *International Journal of Bilingualism* 14: 37–64.

Raschka, C., Li Wei & Lee, S. 2002. Bilingual development and social networks of British-born Chinese children. *International Journal of the Sociology of Language* 153: 9–25.

Roberts, J., Krakow, R. & Pollock, K. 2003. Language outcomes for preschool children adopted from China as infants and toddlers. *Journal of Multilingual Communication Disorders* 1: 177–183.

Tabors, P. 2008. *One child, two languages. A guide for early childhood educators of children learning English as a second language* (2nd ed.). Baltimore: Paul H. Brooks.

Xiao, Y. 2002. The syntactic development of school-age Chinese-speaking children learning English. IRAL *International Review of Applied Linguistics in Language Teaching* 40: 235–271.

Yang, Hsueh-Yin & Zhu Hua. 2010. The phonological development of a trilingual child: facts and factors. In *BAMFLA (Bilingual and Multilingual First Language Acquisition) of Chinese children*, Li Wei (ed.), A special issue of the *International Journal of Bilingualism* 14: 105–126.

Yip, V. & Matthews, S. 2007. *The Bilingual Child: Early Development and Language Contact*. Cambridge: CUP.

Zhu Hua. 2002. *Phonological Development in Specific Contexts: Studies of Chinese-speaking Children*. Clevedon: Multilingual Matters.

Zhu Hua & Li Wei. 1999. Stylistic variation in the early lexical development of young Putonghua-speaking children. *Asia-Pacific Journal of Speech, Language and Hearing* 4: 39–51.

"The more languages, the more English?"

A Dutch perspective

Jacomine Nortier
Utrecht University, the Netherlands

This article explores the empirical basis for the publicly expressed impressions and feelings that the impact and importance of English are a threat to the status and use of Dutch. This is done by looking at various linguistic and sociolinguistic phenomena. Among these, for instance, are the integration of English loan words into Dutch, the use of English in Dutch advertising and the use of English within the context of European Union meetings in Brussels. Although in some situations Dutch is indeed losing out to English, the overall finding is that contrary to public opinion Dutch is by no means in danger.

Introduction

This article focuses on the relation between Dutch as used in the Netherlands and other languages, in particular English. In order to sketch this relation, it is necessary to know what the position of Dutch is within and beyond Dutch borders. The central question to be answered is: is Dutch losing ground in favor of English?

The first section gives an impression of the influence of English on everyday Dutch, and of the attitudes that people have towards the increasing use of English, particularly in the lexicon. The next section shows how English lexical elements are integrated into Dutch and thus have become part of it. In Section 3 the use of English in Dutch advertising will be discussed. Section 4 briefly concentrates on the situation of Dutch abroad, outside the Dutch speaking countries. In Section 5, the contact situation of Dutch and English is compared to other contact situations that have been described in the literature. I will show that for Dutch to change or lose its identity, more is needed than the influence that English has had on Dutch in the past few decades. In the final section, the situation of Dutch as a small language in the European government context is described. Amongst others, I will report on an interview on this topic that I had with an EU interpreter in Brussels.

In this article, the description is limited to Dutch as the main language of the Netherlands, although it is also used as the main language in a large part of Belgium (Flanders).

1.   English and everyday Dutch

In the Netherlands (and Flanders), a lot of people are worried about the ever increasing influence of English. They fear that Dutch will disappear in the end, and that English will take over its position. How realistic is this fear? How serious is the threat? Is it possible at all to give an objective analysis of the rivalry between Dutch and English, if any?

The *Stichting Taalverdediging* (Foundation for Language Defense; see http://www.taalverdediging.nl/) is firmly convinced that the position and use of Dutch has to be actively defended. One of their activities is to propose alternative Dutch words for more than 1,000 English words that have become common usage in the Netherlands. For many of those words, it seems reasonable to replace them with already existing Dutch equivalents, such as *bijlage* for *attachment*, or *springen* for *jumpen*. Both the Dutch words and their English equivalents here are commonly used and, importantly, have more or less the same connotations. Thus, for these borrowings there is no lexical gap in Dutch that could explain the importation from English.

I am sure, however, there are also many of the Stichting's proposals for Dutch that will never be taken seriously; they will only be made fun of, either because the English word has already been fully accepted, or because the English and Dutch words have different connotations. This is confirmed by a small informal investigation among friends, colleagues and students. Examples are the neologisms *schopboksen* for *kickboxing, papierklemmetje* for *paperclip* and *pluimbal* for *badminton*. These three English origin words are fully accepted in Dutch and their Dutch equivalents sound odd for many speakers of Dutch.

Sometimes, the English loanwords have a meaning that is slightly different from their closest Dutch equivalents. An example is the existing Dutch word *geboortegolf*, which is being proposed as a replacement for English *baby boom*. A *geboortegolf* (literally meaning *birth wave*), however, may have taken place anytime in the past, present or future. The term *baby boom*, however, specifically refers to the first years after the Second World War in which the birth rate increased dramatically. In Dutch we refer to people who now (2010) are in their early or mid sixties as *baby boomers*.

Another difference is the one between English *aerobics* and the proposed Dutch neologism *snelgymnastiek* (literally meaning *fast gymnastics* – which in turn is borrowed from Greek). I think few people would consider aerobics to be a way of doing gymnastics in a fast way.

In my opinion, the examples show that such attempts to purify Dutch cannot be expected to be successful outside the group of people who are active within the Stichting Taalverdediging since many (though not all) proposals are unrealistic and do not consider actual usage. Also, the proposals often fail to recognize that linguistic integration already has taken place.

English plays a role not only in the very words that are used in Dutch. In the Netherlands there are many levels of society in which English is being used for communication. This is especially the case in higher education. At Dutch universities, some classes are taught in English, in particular at the Master's level. This is also the case outside departments of English. In international groups, the lingua franca is always English. The presence of one person who does not understand Dutch is enough for everyone else to change the language used from Dutch into English. But even when there is no overt necessity, English is sometimes used. I attended a symposium where attendance was open to an international audience. All participants turned out to speak and understand Dutch. In spite of this, however, the language used was English. This situation is not exceptional.

Also at the secondary level English has started to play an important role in the Netherlands. So called Bilingual Secondary Schools are becoming increasingly popular. In these schools, both Dutch and English are the languages of instruction. In fact, the term "bilingual education" almost exclusively refers to education in which Dutch and English (and German, but only in one school in the city of Venlo) are the languages of instruction.

Dutch students have to learn some German and French in secondary education, but for the most only up to a very modest level. In 2003, a secondary school in Utrecht tried to introduce Turkish as an obligatory part of the curriculum but had to withdraw the plan after strong protests, mainly by parents and outsiders. In the first part of November 2003, there was a fierce discussion in local and national newspapers and on the Internet about the pros and in particular the cons of this plan (see, for example, the newspapers *Utrechts Nieuwsblad*, *De Volkskrant*, and the forum http://forums.marokko.nl/archive/index.php/t-171031.html).

English is also taught in primary schools. However, in contrast to bilingual schools, at primary schools English is taught as a foreign language and not used as the language of instruction. This is also the case at 'ordinary' secondary schools. Starting at age 10–11 (the seventh grade in the Dutch school system), English classes are compulsory. There is a tendency, however, to start with English at a younger age, sometimes even before age six. Early Bird is the program used for the teaching of English to primary school children. For the very young there is Early Birdie (see www.earlybirdie.nl; this site contains information on Early Bird as well).

To summarize, English is sometimes used where Dutch could fulfill the same role, but within the Dutch linguistic system, influence from English is superficial and almost exclusively lexical. These were just some examples of how English has become a part of life in the Netherlands or maybe even: a part of Dutch. In the next section, linguistic integration of English origin lexical material into Dutch will be discussed at more length.

2.   The linguistic integration of English loan words

Many originally English words have become part of Dutch and are fully integrated as regards their structure. They are so to say wrapped into Dutch morphology, such as *jumpen* above, with the Dutch *-en* infinitive ending attached to the English stem *jump*. Other Dutch suffixes are also easily used with English stems, such as the diminutive *-(t)je*: *een filetje* (a small file). Another example is *-e*, which is used on almost all attributively used adjectives: *coole muziek* (cool music). I recently saw a computer game advertised with '*coole gerenderde graphics*' (cool rendered graphics). In *gerenderde*, the discontinuous participle morpheme *ge-/-d* is combined with the adjective *-e* ending. The free morpheme here, *render*, is an import from English. Other examples of frequently used integrated loans in a Dutch participle frame are *gedownload, gecancelled, geformat* and *geskipt* (based, repectively, on the English verbs *download, cancel, format* and *skip*). The participle form derived from English *deleted* is quite commonly used in spoken Dutch but there is no consensus as to how it should be written: *gedelete? gedeleet?* Dutch *gedeleerd* is also used but less common. In *gedelete*, (only) English writing conventions for the stem *delete* are preserved. *Gedeleet* or *gedelet* would be a problem in written Dutch. Since the Dutch rules are followed in these cases, obviously, readers would expect the vowels <e> or <ee> to have a Dutch pronunciation, too (as in English *cave*). In order to be consistent with both spelling and pronunciation rules in Dutch, actually *gedieliet* would be the only right way of spelling it. I have never encountered this form, however. There seems to be a preference for some kind of hybrid form in which the English root can be recognized.

In Dutch, both *-s* and *-en* can be used as plural suffixes, depending on the characteristics of the last syllable. In English, however, only *-s* is possible. I overheard some girls going to town in order to buy *stringen* which in English would have been *strings*.

Not only English morphology but also the pronunciation of English origin words in Dutch is adjusted to Dutch, both on the segmental and suprasegmental levels. This is not true for all loan words but there are examples such as *corned beef* which is pronounced as [kɔrnɛt biːf]. A *penalty* is pronounced as *penàlty* in Dutch, and is only used in soccer.

It is characteristic of loan words that they are used both by those who speak the imported language and those who do not. However, the number of people in the Netherlands without any knowledge of English is dramatically decreasing. Yet there are still people in the Netherlands who do not speak any English. Like those who do know English, they go out to *shoppen* instead of *winkelen* but I am not sure whether they prefer to buy their stuff in a *sale* instead of in the old-fashioned *uitverkoop* (cf. Field 2002).

No wonder that people in the Netherlands are worried about the position of Dutch and the threat from English. They fear that English will take over the position of Dutch and that would be the end of our own national identity. On their website, the Stichting Taalverdediging has stated that if we continue to allow "Englishisation/Americanisation" to attack Dutch, we will have to conclude in the end that it was our own fault, but then it will be too late to intervene. We have to fight against English and with the help of us all, the Stichting Taalverdediging will be able to do something about it. We as Dutch people have to be convinced that we have a full-fledged, mature language that, just like Dutch soil, should not be overruled by forces from the west.[1]

Does this way of thinking show how closely language and identity are tied together in the perception of speakers of Dutch? I think it is not that simple. In order to see the influence of English in a broader perspective, I would like to take a look at the use of Dutch by emigrants abroad.

3.   Dutch abroad

In typical immigrant countries such as Australia, New-Zealand and Canada, Dutch is one of the first languages whose daily use is replaced by the language of the new country, although this does not always mean that Dutch is diluted or forgotten (cf. de Bot & Clyne 1994). In most cases, the new language is English. It is not uncommon for Dutch to disappear in immigrant homes within fewer than

1. My rendering of the main ideas expressed in "Als we met lede ogen blijven toezien hoe de bedreiging van het Nederlands door de verengelsing/veramerikaansing om zich heen grijpt, zullen we over een aantal jaren moeten vaststellen dat het onze eigen schuld is geweest. Het is zaak er nu tegenin te gaan en de onzin aan de kaak te stellen. Daarvoor is de Stichting Taal-verdediging opgericht en we zijn ervan overtuigd dat er samen met u heel wat te bereiken is. Laten we beseffen dat we een volwaardige taal hebben die net zo min als ons grondgebied mag bezwijken onder de vloed uit het westen" on the site www.taalverdediging.nl.

two generations, while other immigrants, such as Germans or Vietnamese, maintain their original languages much longer (cf. Smolicz 1992).

This difference has to do with the place that language takes in a hierarchy of ethnic core values (Smolicz 1992). Stated here in a strongly simplified manner, these are values without which individuals do not consider themselves (or are not considered by others) to be members of a certain ethnic group. Some values are more precious to the members of the group than other ones. For example, in order to be identified as a Frisian, speaking Frisian is more important than being protestant or drinking Beerenburger brandy. In the town of Holland, Michigan (United States), which was founded by Dutch immigrants, many typically Dutch cultural elements have been preserved or re-invented, houses have been built in a Dutch style, there is a Dutch wind mill, and Dutch tulips are grown, but the use of the Dutch language is not common, due to the low position it has in the hierarchy of ethnic core values. The same seems to be the case with Berber. Bentahila and Davies (1988) mention in a paper on language shift among Berbers in Morocco:

> None of those who were not fluent in Berber reported that their parents were particularly disturbed by this; typical was a girl who remarked that her father was more upset at her wearing of European-style clothes than at the fact that she had forgotten her Berber!   Bentahila and Davies (1988: 3)

The fact that Dutch emigrants attach more value to expressions of their ethnic belonging other than language does not necessarily mean that Dutch is in danger. Dutch is only changing positions with English (or another language, of course) in situations in which language shift is taking place anyway, irrespective of which language is at stake. The position of language in a hierarchy of ethnic core values only explains why Dutch is disappearing faster than some other languages in immigrant situations but it does not make any predictions about the linguistic situation within the Netherlands.

Although Dutch may disappear quickly among emigrants, it is quite alive as a foreign language *extra muros*. There are 258 schools outside the Netherlands and Flanders where Dutch is used as the language of instruction (see http://www.stichtingnob.nl/index_real.jsp). Dutch can be studied as a language at 220 universities in 46 countries outside the Netherlands and Flanders, in virtually all continents. In the German city of Munster there are even more students of Dutch than there are university students of German in the Netherlands.

4. Advertisements

Lexical influence from another language is not restricted to the present and it is not unique. In the more recent past, Dutch has undergone strong lexical influence from, amongst others, French, which was highly prestigious until far into the past century. Any page in a Dutch dictionary will still show more French than English-origin lemmas.

Just as English is frequently used for commercial purposes these days, advertisements in the beginning of the twentieth century frequently made use of French in order to attract buyers. Here is the text from an advertisement for a fashionable dress by the Dutch department store De Bijenkorf in 1925, taken from De Vries and van Amstel (1974; French origin words in italics):

> *Casaque*, lang model, van kunstzijde, *ramagé dessins*.
> (*Casaque*, long style, artificial silk, *decorated (with) designs*)

Or what to think of this one, from 1917 or 1918:

> *Bébémantel met pelerine, prima witte batist gegarneerd met broderie anglaise.*
> (Baby coat with cape, excellent white fine cotton, decorated with English embroidery)

Nowadays, it is English that is popular in advertisements. Could it be the case that slogans are more attractive when they are in English? Examples are *"Let's make things better"*, *"Getting you there"*, *"Life is for sharing"*, *"Ideas for life!"* or *"Coole hippy styles!"* (with the Dutch adjective ending -*e* inserted in *coole*). It seems that products and services make a more global or transnational and, therefore, better, impression when the potential buyer can see that they have an international flavor instead of local Dutch.

Renkema, Vallen and Hoeken (2003) discuss the use of English in advertisements in the Netherlands. They describe the results of a study from the late nineties which revealed that 15% of the advertisements on Dutch television directed towards a Dutch audience were in English. At the same time, a survey among Dutch informants showed that the English words used in advertisements are not always fully understood. In addition, the use of English is not considered as something particularly positive or attractive. In another study it was shown that the appreciation of the use of English in advertisements depends on the type of product that is advertised for. Typically Dutch products (like a birthday calendar or a cheese slicer) should not use English in their advertisements, while it is less problematic when international products (such as Levi's) are being promoted.

In their article, Renkema et al. (2003) tried to answer the question why the use of English in advertisements is increasing although at the same time it is being criticized. The authors set up an experiment at the University of Tilburg in order to investigate whether English slogans and terms used in advertisements for services, products and job vacancies and their Dutch equivalents might show semantic differences. In order to do so they paired up Dutch and English slogans and terms that were more or less equivalent, or, in any case, as much as possible so. Some examples are:

(1) a. *The spirit of freshness* versus *De geest van frisheid*
     b. *(…) coachen, supporten van (…) communication consultants* [van = of]
         versus *(…) begeleiden, ondersteunen van (…) communicatie adviseurs*

The outcome was that it did not seem to make much difference to the informants whether English or Dutch was used in advertising texts. English was not considered to be more prestigious than Dutch. The informants did find English shop names more attractive than Dutch names (e.g., English *gift shop* versus Dutch *cadeauwinkel*) but this did not influence their overall evaluation of the shop itself. The image did not depend on the use of an English or Dutch name. In names, both languages were found natural, which means that informants have got used to English names. In job advertisements, however, Dutch was found to be more natural than English.

Quite unexpectedly, there was no difference in the way that older or younger people reacted. The results show that there is no special prestige attached to the use of English in advertisements. This indicates that the increasing use of English can only partly (at most) be explained on the basis of semantic differences between Dutch and English equivalents. The effect originally intended by the use of English in advertising (i.e., connotations of exclusivity, being cosmopolitan, being international) is paling not because the use of English or its attractiveness is declining, but because of the opposite: it has become 'normal' and therefore is not suitable anymore for attention-seeking purposes in advertising.

5.   Grammatical change through language contact?

Although it is often feared that Dutch will be overruled by English, there are people who have a much more optimistic view. According to those (and I am one of them), the position of Dutch in the Netherlands is strong. English is unmistakably moving up as a second language, but Dutch remains the native language of millions of native Dutch and Flemish people. For those people, Dutch is the language in which they normally communicate both in formal and informal situations. Moreover, the influence of English is superficial and almost exclusively lexical, as was shown in the section above. The heart of a language is its structure, its grammar, and Dutch grammar does not seem to be affected by English. For grammatical borrowing to occur, centuries of intense contact are a prerequisite. Such situations are for instance found in the Balkans, where grammatical features such as the use of postnominal articles are widespread in a number of genetically related and unrelated languages (Appel & Muysken 1987). This phenomenon possibly originates from Albanian, and has spread through neighboring languages such as Bulgarian, Macedonian, Romanian and Serbian as a consequence of longstanding intensive contact. Romanian is a Romance language, Bulgarian, Serbian and Macedonian are Slavic languages and they all have adopted postnominal articles (Appel & Muysken 1987: 155).

It is hard to imagine that Dutch could undergo deep grammatical influence from English, like for example the adoption of third singular *-s* on the inflected verb. This seems to be impossible at the moment since all influence that has been observed so far has been restricted to the lexical level. However, we don't know what will happen in the long run.

According to some linguists, there is grammatical change going on in Dutch (Weerman 2003; van Ginkel 2006; van der Hoek 2005; Unsworth 2008; Hulk & Cornips 2006). This change concerns the nominal system for singular NP's, where neuter gender is becoming more and more marked in favor of the unmarked common gender (Dutch does not mark gender on plural NP's). The overuse of common gender is visible in the use of definite articles and attributively used demonstratives and adjectives. Definite articles are *de* (common) and *het* (neuter). Demonstrative pronouns are *deze/die* (common) and *dit/dat* (neuter). Adjectives that are used attributively have an *-e* ending, except in indefinite neuter NP's. This is illustrated in Table 1.

Table 2 shows a recent overgeneralization of common gender where traditionally neuter nouns are treated as if they had common gender.

Table 1. Gender in Dutch determiners and attributive adjectives

Singular NP's	Common gender	Neuter gender
Definite	De goede fiets	Het goede huis
	The good bicycle	*The good house*
Indefinite	Een goede fiets	Een goed huis
	A good bicycle	*A good house*
Demonstrative	Deze/die goede fiets	Dit/dat goede huis
	This/that good bicycle	*This/that good house*

Table 2. Overgeneralization of common gender in Dutch

	Common gender	Traditionally neuter gender
Definite	De goede fiets	De goede huis
	The good bicycle	*The good house*
Indefinite	Een goede fiets	Een goede huis
	A good bicycle	*A good house*
Demonstrative	Deze/die goede fiets	Deze/die goede huis
	This/that good bicycle	*This/that good house*

Superficially, the overuse of *de* (common gender) at the cost of *het* (neuter gender) looks as if it is influenced by English, since Dutch *de* and English *the* sound more or less the same.

A more plausible explanation, however, is not specifically based on contact with English, but on the acquisition of Dutch as a second language. Van der Hoek (2005) convincingly showed that the way bilingual children acquire grammatical gender is different from monolingual Dutch children, and therefore, their use of grammatical gender is different. The bilingual children in her study did not acquire both languages as if they were first languages. Rather, they learned Dutch as a second language outside their homes. Other studies of second language acquisition suggest that the rules about the use of adjective ending -*e* are acquired relatively late. Some linguists believe that in second language acquisition, the rule is not only acquired relatively late but sometimes not at all, i.e., all attributively used adjectives have -*e*, including the cases where they are combined with indefinite neuter nouns (cf., e.g., Van der Velde 2003). Some forms of substandard Dutch in which second language learner variations such as the incorrect use of nominal gender are included have strong covert prestige, which might explain their spread to native speakers as well (Weerman 2003).

6.   Dutch, the global language system and Eurobarometer

When people do not speak and understand each other's (native) languages, usually they try to find a common language, a *lingua franca* (e.g., Knapp & Meierkord 2002 and the contributions by Kohn and Seidlhofer, this volume). In practice, this role is increasingly fulfilled by English (ibid.). Sociologist de Swaan (2001: 144) rightly observed: "The more languages, the more English". Internationally he sees a unique role for English.

De Swaan explains what he calls "the global language system", a worldwide constellation of languages. In this constellation, four levels can be distinguished. The vast majority of the five or six thousand languages spoken on earth, 98%, are situated on the lowest level. These are the 'peripheral' languages. Although there are thousands of them, they are used by less than ten per cent of mankind. Many of them have no written form.

Contact between groups who speak peripheral languages is only possible when they have learned a common second language, called a central language. The peripheral languages are grouped around this central language. The central languages are used in education and in bureaucracy, and they are written. They may function as national languages. Some examples are Dutch in the Netherlands or Yoruba in Nigeria.

At a higher level, de Swaan (2001) positions a few supercentral languages that are used for international communication. Examples are Arabic, Chinese, Russian and Spanish. But if an Arab, a Chinese and a Russian or other speakers of supercentral languages meet, there is a fair chance that they will use the only language that connects them. This language currently is English, and de Swaan calls it "the hypercentral language". Contact between languages on different levels is only possible through bilinguals.

Characteristic of the constellation proposed by de Swaan is that second (third, etc.) languages are predominantly learned unidirectionally, i.e., the language usually learned is a language higher up in the hierarchy. For instance, it is unusual (though not impossible) for native speakers of a supercentral language to learn a second language from a central or peripheral level. If they learn a new language, a language that is situated at a higher level such as English will be the most probable candidate. The higher a language is situated in the constellation, the higher the probability that it will (also) be learned as a second (third, etc.) language. This means that a native speaker of Standard Dutch will not actively learn a lower status variety such as the dialect from Limburg or the Achterhoek but preferably a language higher up in De Swaan's hierarchy, such as French, German or English. In choosing the hypercentral language English, the level of the supercentral languages French and German is skipped.

But English is far from the only foreign language that is being used in the Netherlands today.

The so called Eurobarometer is a public opinion analysis instrument which is updated and published on a regular basis. Data have been and are being collected among tens of thousands of Europeans.[2] Eurobarometer 2006 has revealed that an average of 28% of EU-citizens use two or more languages in addition to their

---

2. The standard Eurobarometer was established in 1973. Each survey consists of approximately 1000 face-to-face interviews per Member State (except Germany: 1500, Luxembourg: 600, United Kingdom 1300 including 300 in Northern Ireland). It is conducted between 2 and 5 times per year, with reports published twice yearly (http://ec.europa.eu).

mother tongue. In the Netherlands, the average was 75%, but Luxemburgers beat all others with 93%. According to the same Eurobarometer, Utrecht is the third multilingual hotspot in Europe (after Malta and Luxemburg). This is not because a large number of different languages are spoken, but it has to do with the fact that individuals are proficient in a great number of languages. 77% of the population in Utrecht is able to speak three languages or more; 8% even speak more than five languages (however, there is no information on levels of language proficiency; see http://ec.europa.eu/education/languages/pdf/doc3822_en.pdf).

The explanation for these high percentages in Utrecht may be found in demographic factors: the population is relatively young, there are institutions for higher education that attract students from abroad, and there is a considerable group of (former) labor migrants.

It is European policy to encourage all Europeans to be able to communicate in two languages other than their native tongue (http://ec.europa.eu/education/languages/pdf/doc3822_en.pdf). In this respect, Utrecht is doing a good European job.

In the 2006 version of the Eurobarometer it is also shown that English is the number one foreign language in Europe.[3] 38% of EU-citizens who were interviewed stated that their English is proficient enough to use it in a conversation. Among Dutch respondents, as many as 87% reported to speak English as a

---

3. At the same time that English has been on the rise as the first foreign language in Europe, the relative number of native speakers of English in Europe has been decreasing. English as an L1 is far from threatened but in the British media a growing concern can be observed. An example is the publication of *English Next* by David Gradoll in 2006. In this publication, he expresses the need for L1 speakers of English to learn other languages as well:

> David Graddol concludes that monoglot English graduates face a bleak economic future as qualified multilingual youngsters from other countries are proving to have a competitive advantage over their British counterparts in global companies and organisations. Alongside that, many countries are introducing English into the primary curriculum but – to say the least – British schoolchildren and students do not appear to be gaining greater encouragement to achieve fluency in other languages.
>
> If left to themselves, such trends will diminish the relative strength of the English language in international education markets as the demand for educational resources in languages, such as Spanish, Arabic or Mandarin grows and international business process outsourcing in other languages such as Japanese, French and German, spreads.   (Graddol 2006: fragment from Foreword, p. 1)

And also:

> Global English has led to a crisis of terminology. The distinctions between 'native speaker', 'second-language speaker', and 'foreign-language user' have become blurred.
>   (Graddol 2006: 110)

second language (http://ec.europa.eu/public_opinion/archives/ebs/ebs_243_
sum_nl.pdf). Again, it is unknown what the respondents' English proficiency
levels are.

None of this has any immediate consequences for Dutch in itself, but the
question can be asked whether the Dutch are as proficient in English as they often seem to believe. In the following section, an interpreter in Brussels sheds her
light on the position of Dutch in Europe, including the Dutch and their (lack of)
proficiency in English.

7.   An interpreter in Brussels: Dutch as a small language among other languages in the European Union

Officially, all 23 languages of the European Union are also working languages.
There is a big apparatus to deal with them at official meetings. One of the necessary consequences is that the European Parliament has its own interpreters. The
Secretary of the Council of Europe has a certain amount of money available for
each language and each country to spend on interpretations and translations. This
money is made available twice a year.

Every sixth months (the length of a chairmanship) the civil servants of the
permanent representative of a country indicate in which meetings they need
active (to language X) or passive (from language X to another language) interpretation. If more is needed, it is paid for by the relevant individual countries
themselves.

For the meetings of the European Commission, the ECOSOC (Economic and
Social Council) and the Regional Comittee, interpreters are used according to
the so called 'besoins réels' ('real needs'). These are established on the basis of the
combination of the following factors: the level of importance of a certain meeting,
the language needs/wishes of the delegates and the presence of (sufficient) cabins
(for the interpreters) in the conference rooms.

In the beginning of 2009, I had an interview with a Dutch interpreter who
works for the EU in Brussels. We talked about the use of Dutch, English and other
languages in EU meetings and among fellow interpreters:

> We [EU interpreters] always work in meetings. There are meetings without Dutch
> interpreters, and the Budget Committee is an example (although I am not even
> sure about that since per definition, I am never present during meetings without
> Dutch interpreters). Sometimes, when the Permanent Representative has applied
> for it, the Dutch and Flemish are allowed to speak Dutch during the meetings.
> And then there may be interpreters in the other cabins (English, German, French,
> Spanish, for example) who have Dutch 'passively', i.e., they understand Dutch,

but it isn't their native language. It may be the case that there is no room for passive Dutch in such meetings. In those cases Dutch and Flemish delegates have to speak another language, like English or German. It is sometimes difficult to understand for outsiders that the presence of Dutch speaking interpreters (in our case about fifty/fifty Dutch and Flemish) has nothing to do with being allowed to speak Dutch but only with the right to listen to a translation into Dutch.

(Translation from Dutch by the author.
The original text appeared in Nortier 2009: 25–26)

The demand for interpreters differs per country. France, for example, requires interpreters for almost every meeting while other countries such as the Netherlands have a more reserved attitude. This is mainly due to delegates' knowledge of other languages, which in general is higher among the Dutch delegates in Brussels than among the French. Besides, national pride plays a role, too. This pride is relatively strong among the French, in comparison to the average Dutch delegates who easily switch to other languages than their own. Exactly this attitude is at the heart of the fears of possible language – and identity – loss!

Interpreters amongst themselves

Informal contact between interpreters does not always take place in English, which might have been the expected *lingua franca*. After all, English is moving up as the language of globalization, and also within the Netherlands the use of English is increasing. All interpreters are by definition proficient in a number of languages. For Dutch and Flemish interpreters this adds up to four or five foreign languages, and some of them even speak more. Only few of them (usually newcomers) speak fewer than four to five foreign languages. Interpreters from the new member states usually do not speak more than one or two foreign languages. Language use amongst interpreters may therefore vary, as is explained in the next paragraph.

My informant, who is a native speaker of Dutch, has Danish, French, Swedish and English as her working languages from which she interprets into Dutch. When she talks with a Danish interpreter, they use Danish, and only when there is no other common language, a major language like English or French is chosen. Among themselves, interpreters often use a (what they call) 'exotic' or small language, such as Greek, Bulgarian, Finnish or Dutch. As was mentioned already, sometimes they choose to use French or English when it is the only language they have in common.

Contrary to the situation in the Netherlands where English is the most commonly used foreign language, the interpreters in Brussels in the first place use the languages they have in common. Since interpreters are proficient in more than two languages, the chances that they share and, therefore, use other languages than English are higher than among 'ordinary' people.

I expected speakers of small or 'exotic' languages to feel some kind of solidarity with each other, but that does not seem to be the case. Speaking a small language plays a marginal role. Solidarity is not achieved through the status or size of one's native language. Shared cultural and social values are considered to be more important.

Although smaller languages are used among interpreters, the larger the group of interpreters speaking to each other, the more chance that English is chosen as a lingua franca. This has in particular been the case since the new Eastern and Middle European members entered the EU, because in general, English is the first foreign language known by Middle and Eastern European interpreters. There are exceptions: the Romanians usually have French as their first foreign language and for the Czechs the first foreign (EU) language often is German. Russian was the most important second language during the Soviet era, but nowadays the younger generation does not speak Russian anymore and besides: Russian is not an EU language.

Even the French, who used to reject the use of other languages than French, nowadays use more English than ten or fifteen years ago. Spanish interpreters also speak English in informal conversation, although it still is the case that Romance languages are preferred above English in contacts with Southern European interpreters. The reason is, according to my informant, that Spanish, Italian, French and Portuguese are all related Romance languages. She was not aware of scientific research concerning language choice but it was her impression that in Southern European countries the relatively poor knowledge and use of English is increasing now, because it is taught on a larger scale and also because teaching methods have improved. Moreover, for commercial and tourist reasons the South-Europeans consider English to be more important now than in the past.

All interpreters who have been in Brussels for several years speak English and French, even when they are not their working languages. Contrary to ten or twenty years ago, their proficiency in both languages is high enough to facilitate communicate with other interpreters, according to the interpreter who was interviewed.

Languages in EU meetings

In EU-meetings English is now being used more than ever before. If everyone were to use their own official language, there would be 23 languages in use at the same time. That would very complicated but there are situations where it is necessary, e.g., when the Council of Ministers has its official meetings. During several other meetings, however, there is a 'restricted language regime'. In practice this means that, for example, ten languages are being spoken and six cabins with interpreters are used. As a consequence, for instance, the Dutch are allowed to speak Dutch, but there is no interpretation available into Dutch. Therefore, they will have to choose another language such as English in order to understand what, say, a Czech speaker is saying. In such situations the Dutch often switch to the active use of English. Not surprisingly, hearing English often leads to speaking it, too. Another possibility would be, however, that each person speaks their own language regardless of what others speak, as long as they are able to understand each other. This form of communication is called *receptive bilingualism*. According to the people who communicate in a receptive bilingual way, it costs some effort to stick to one's own language in the beginning, but it has great advantages, obviously (cf. Ten Thije & Zeevaert 2007).

The use of interpreters is only partly a matter of the ability and willingness to pay for these expensive services. Paying for interpreters is also a matter of priorities and principles. British delegates listen exclusively to English for the simple reason that in general, they do not understand any other EU working language.

When the Dutch do not get interpreters during meetings, for whatever reason, they usually accept English without any protest. But when Spain entered the EU, there were not enough interpreters to translate from and into Spanish. Sometimes complete meetings were cancelled by the Spanish delegates. They demanded interpreters, and threatened to leave the meeting if their demands were not met. The cancellation of meetings and the arranging of new meetings is extremely costly so it did not take long before enough Spanish interpreters were available. Spain and Portugal became EU members at the same time. Even though the Portuguese sometimes also encountered linguistic problems, and there were not always Portuguese interpreters available, in contrast to their neighbors, they never cancelled any meetings because of a lack of interpreters.

As has become clear from these anecdotes, speakers of the major languages may be more demanding than speakers of smaller or 'exotic' languages. Even if the delegates of larger or more influential countries speak and understand English, they often will not use it and will ask for interpreters. Dutch delegates, on the contrary, often have an attitude of 'Look how fluent my English is' or 'I don't want to cause any trouble'. This attitude is shared with the Scandinavians.

Since the majority of Middle and Eastern European members joined the EU only recently, there is still a lack of interpreters with a good command of Middle and Eastern European languages (as foreign languages). It is only recently that interpreters from Western-European countries have started to learn Middle and

Eastern European languages. A lot of work is being done to solve that problem. Years before the Middle and Eastern European members entered the EU, additional courses in Czech, Polish, Hungarian etc. were organized for the Western European interpreters, but they still lag behind.

In general, it can be said that the Dutch and Flemish delegates speak Dutch whenever they are allowed to during official occasions in Brussels, i.e., when their interlocutors who speak other native languages have interpreters available. Besides, Dutch and Flemish delegates speak English very well, or at least, they think they do...

The Dutch newspaper *De Volkskrant* reported on 20 October, 2005, about the misunderstandings resulting from Dutch delegates working at the EU who pretended they could do without an interpreter:

> According to the Belgian representative Bart Staes, the Dutch are inclined to switch to English, also in EU meetings. They tend to overestimate their knowledge of English. He remembered a Dutch civil servant who said during the closing session at the end of a long and intense meeting: *'Let's continue this meeting tomorrow, because today we have hardly worked'*. Staes understood what the speaker wanted to say (*'we worked hard'*) but what would a French or Latvian interpreter have made of it? Another civil servant talked about the gas deposits in the North of the country: *'We have gas in our bottom'*.
>
> Two million euros are reserved for interpreters for each language per 6 month period. It is striking that the Flemish make much more use of this service than the Dutch.   (Text shortened and translated by the author)

As indicated earlier, the choice of languages used at meetings does not only depend on financial considerations, or actual linguistic knowledge of the delegates, but also on the status that a certain meeting has. During meetings of the Council of Ministers all participants use their own language, even when they speak other languages as well. In important and highly prestigious meetings, the choice for a particular language is politically motivated. At less prestigious meetings interpreters may be needed but interpretation at these meetings is often considered less important at a political level.

On rare occasions sign language interpreters are involved in the meetings in Brussels, but usually only when matters related to the Deaf Community are concerned. For example, at such meetings speaking interpreters will translate from French into Dutch and signing interpreters will translate from Dutch into Dutch Sign Language (Nederlandse Gebarentaal).

The small languages

In Europe, Dutch is a relatively 'small' language and English is an example of a 'big' language (but see Wilton & De Houwer, this volume). This can be noticed when at official meetings the British (and, partly, the Irish) always use their own languages, which seems to be a right of the big languages. Besides, there are always interpreters available, which the Dutch do not have when there is a 'restricted language regime'(as mentioned above). Dutch delegates listen to other languages such as English, German or French, when Dutch is not available. As mentioned before: English is used by both natives and non-natives; Dutch only by native speakers.

When the European Commission presents a proposal for a new regulation, it is usually in English. The next step is that the Commission and civil servants of the member states discuss the proposal. Then counterproposals are formulated and discussed and so forth. All together it may take years before a decision is taken. In the course of the process, translations are provided. In the end, the regulation is available in all 23 official EU working languages.

First versions of documents are almost always formulated in English and never in Dutch or other small languages. For the Dutch this is not a severe problem, but in countries where the majority of people have great problems with English, this might cause some trouble.

Speakers of big languages are more visible and 'hearable' than speakers of the 'smaller' languages. This is not only because they want to be seen or heard but mainly because they really do not understand any other languages.[4] Alternatively, delegates who meet in Brussels may be able to speak and understand another language, but when they return to their home countries with the results of their negotiations in order to discuss them with colleagues or specialists, they may encounter serious problems when the documents are only available in a language that the majority of the people back home do not understand.

In the beginning of this section, it was stated that the 23 official languages of the EU are also working languages. It has become clear from the interview with the Dutch interpreter, however, that the practical situation is different. Not only are some languages more privileged than others, for many reasons, the situation is very complex, too. Attitudes, history, and aspects of multilingualism together determine the usefulness and popularity of each language.

---

4. Cf. the aforementioned upward learnability of languages in the language constellation as proposed by Abram de Swaan.

8.   Conclusion

The question as to whether Dutch is running the risk of being overruled by English can be answered with a firm no. Above, I showed that English is gaining influence in many areas. The Dutch love bilingualism, but only as long as one language is Dutch and the other one is English. We should be realistic and alert not to use English when Dutch is available, but linguistically the influence from English on Dutch is superficial since it is mainly lexical. Although Dutch continues to adopt many loan words from English, those words are soon incorporated into the Dutch linguistic system, both on the level of pronunciation and grammar.

Dutch is still the main language spoken in Dutch homes and in the broader society. Many who fear the power of English seem to have forgotten that other languages have been very influential in the past. French is a good example from recent history. The popularity of English now is comparable to the popularity of French in the first half of the twentieth century, as was illustrated in the analysis of advertisements. Dutch has a solid position in the Netherlands.

The fact that Dutch is easily lost in emigrant communities is not new or typical of the present, but has to do with the position language takes in a hierarchy of ethnic core values. Although Dutch quickly disappears from emigrant communities, it does not seem to threaten the future of Dutch anywhere else.

The interview with a Dutch EU interpreter revealed that in the European context, Dutch is a small language. However, that does not mean that it has no importance or value at all. Like other small languages, Dutch takes its own unique position in Europe.

References

Appel, R. & Muysken, P. 1987. *Language Contact and Bilingualism*. London: Edward Arnold.

Bentahila, A. & Davies, E. 1988. Convergence and divergence: Two cases of language shift in Morocco. Paper presented at the *Maintenance and Loss of Ethnic Minority Languages* conference, Noordwijkerhout, the Netherlands.

de Bot, K. & Clyne, M. 1994. A 16-year longitudinal study of language attrition in Dutch immigrants in Australia. *Journal of Multilingual and Multicultural Development* 15: 17–28.

de Swaan, A. 2001. *Words of the World*. Cambridge: Polity Press.

de Vries, L. & van Amstel, I. 1974. *Eene Wandeling door den Bijenkorf*. Amsterdam: De Bijenkorf.

Field, F. 2002. *Linguistic Borrowing in Bilingual Contexts* [Studies in Language Companion Series 62]. Amsterdam: John Benjamins.

Graddol, D. 2006. *English Next. Why Global English May Mean the End of 'English as a Foreign Language'*. British Council. <http://www.britishcouncil.org/learning-research-english-next.pdf>.

Hulk, A. & Cornips, L. 2006. Neuter gender determiners and interface vulnerability in child L2 Dutch. In *Paths of Development in L1 and L2 Acquisition*, S. Unsworth, T. Parodi, A. Sorace & M. Young-Scholten (eds), 107–134. Amsterdam: John Benjamins.

Knapp, K. & Meierkord, C. (eds). 2002. *Lingua Franca Communication*. Frankfurt: Peter Lang.

Nortier, J. 2009. *Nederland Meertalenland*. Amsterdam: Aksant.

Renkema, J., Vallen, E. & Hoeken, H. 2003. Tuinapparatuur of garden equipment? Waarom Nederlanders Engels prefereren. In *Waar gaat het Nederlands naar toe?*, J. Stroop (ed.), 108–113. Amsterdam: Bert Bakker.

Smolicz, J. 1992. Minority languages as core values of ethnic cultures. In *Maintenance and Loss of Minority Languages* [Studies in Bilingualism 1], S. Kroon, K. Jaspaert & W. Fase (eds), 277–305. Amsterdam: John Benjamins.

ten Thije, J. & Zeevaert, L. (eds). 2007. *Receptive Multilingualism and Intercultural Communication: Linguistic Analyses, Language Policies and Didactic Concepts* [Hamburg Studies in Multilingualism 6]. Amsterdam: John Benjamins.

Unsworth, S. 2008. Age and input in the acquisition of grammatical gender in Dutch. *Second Language Research* 24: 365–396.

van der Hoek, M. 2005. Tweede taalverwerving door kinderen. De verwerving van het genderkenmerk in het Nederlands door tweetalige kinderen die opgroeien in meertalige gemeenschappen. MA thesis, Utrecht University.

Van der Velde, M. 2003. Déterminants et pronoms en néerlandais et en français: syntaxe et acquisition. PhD dissertation, Université Paris 8.

van Ginkel, B. 2006. De verwerving van lexicale en morfologisch bepaald geslacht. Een onderzoek naar tweede taalverwerving bij eentalige Nederlandse kinderen en tweetalige Turks-Nederlandse kinderen. MA thesis, Utrecht University.

Weerman, F. 2003. Een mooie verhaal. Veranderingen in uitgangen. In *Waar gaat het Nederlands naar toe?*, J. Stroop (ed.), 249–260. Amsterdam: Bert Bakker.

Conceptualizing 'English' for a multilingual Europe

Barbara Seidlhofer
University of Vienna, Austria

The growing importance of English in multilingual Europe poses a dilemma: a common language is important for communal integration, but at the same time it is perceived as threatening European multilingualism. Faced with this quandary, it is crucial how 'English' is conceptualized. It is not possible to resolve the dilemma while upholding traditional concepts of European languages essentially mapped onto nation states. Therefore this paper argues for the need to conceptualize English as a Lingua Franca (ELF) that is not subject to established native-speaker norms but can be, and is, appropriated by all its users. Only such conceptualization can result in ELF not competing with the various national languages but rather complementing them as a valuable part of Europeans' multilingual repertoire.

In 1987, Karlfried Knapp published a paper entitled "English as a lingua franca and the teaching of intercultural communication" (Knapp 1987). There are two reasons why it is appropriate for me to mention this paper here. In the first place, it was one of the very earliest discussions of English as a lingua franca, which is also the topic of this present paper. What I have to say follows on from what Karlfried Knapp wrote almost a quarter of a century ago. The second reason why it is appropriate to mention Karlfried's paper is that it was a contribution to a Festschrift in honour of a distinguished and influential scholar. So is mine.

The issues I want to address in this paper have to do with the role and status of English as one of the languages in a multilingual Europe – they are issues I think that will strike a chord in the Knapp mind.

The definition of Europe in socio-political terms as some kind of union or community rather than just a geographical area obviously calls for a corresponding reappraisal of well-entrenched ways of thinking. This is, of course, well understood in the economic domain, where it is accepted that free market forces and the mobility of labour must take precedence over the protection of merely local interests. In education too there is an acceptance that the diversity of values and standards that have represented the individuality of different nation states needs to be reduced to a common framework. So there is a general assumption that if one is to have a community, there has to be some means of establishing unity and counteracting any separatist tendencies. This assumption, however, does not seem to apply when it comes to languages. Here we find that traditional concepts are still very firmly in place. As a consequence, there is a disparity between the pronouncements of policy informed by these concepts and the communicative requirements of the larger European community. But not only do these pronouncements run counter to the principles of commonality and unity upon which the very notion of community depend, they are also at variance with actual reality.

Europe is multilingual in the sense that its constituent countries have different languages within their borders. In short, it exemplifies societal multilingualism. This does not mean, however, that its citizens are themselves individually multilingual. Far from it. And herein lies the problem. The difference between these two phenomena, the individual and the social, is, of course, well recognised and it has become customary to mark the difference by using the term *plurilingualism* to refer to the former, *multilingualism, tout court,* to refer to the latter. A change of terminology, however, does little to resolve the problem but on the contrary points to the impossibility of its resolution. Given the number of languages in multilingual Europe, it is obvious that its citizens can only hope to be plurilingual in a few of them. And of course, being plurilingual in these will be of no use to individuals if they need to communicate with the innumerable fellow European citizens who do not know them. In spite of this, the rhetoric of educational policy persists in representing plurilingualism as a desirable and feasible objective, and one, furthermore, that is mysteriously achievable by making provision for the teaching of one or two foreign languages at school.

The obvious fact is that individual plurilingualism can never match societal multilingualism and so it can never ever resolve the problem of finding a means for communicating across the diverse linguacultural communities within Europe. The reality is very different from the rhetoric. And the reality is that this communicative role has to a very great extent been taken on by one language, and this language is English.

The fact of the matter is that English has become the de facto 'extraterritorial' lingua franca throughout Europe, 'overarching' several more regional lingua francas. It is firmly established as a language of wider communication, enabling people to link up about common interests, needs and concerns across languages and communities. In this respect, although plurilingualism is often directly associated with inter-culturality, it is English that so often serves as a means of making connections across cultural assumptions and values which, in the absence of a common language of interaction, would otherwise be impossible. And these connections are made in all domains of use by speakers from all levels of society in practically all walks of life.

The importance of this common language for economic globalization is, of course, well established in practice. Due to the internationalization of the economies of European countries, English also forms an integral part of the professional lives of a growing number of Europeans. A significant number of multinational, but also national, companies have adopted English as their company language, no matter whether they have subsidiaries in English-speaking countries or not (Melchers & Shaw 2003:184). The companies do this in order to downplay their national affiliations and position themselves as transnational companies (Truchot 2003:306).

Perhaps the most obvious impact of English in Europe is, however, in the domains of the media, the internet, advertising, popular youth culture and entertainment (Berns, de Bot & Hasebrink 2007; Phillipson 2003; Preisler 1999; Truchot 2002; Pennycook 2007). It is in these domains that English has evidently been spreading beyond the elites. In addition, the (striving for) increased European integration has led to the creation of various informal communication networks and contact situations among "ordinary Europeans" (Labrie & Quell 1997:23). In these situations, English often functions "as a direct mediator between participants in a discourse who would otherwise have to rely on translation or a third party" (Breidbach 2003:20). So English impinges on the lives of all European citizens, in many different ways: academics, business executives and hip hoppers experience the language as a pervasive presence in their daily lives.

In European education systems, English is the most important foreign language taught in its own right from the primary level onwards, and it is increasingly employed in *content-and-language-integrated learning* (CLIL) mainly at the secondary level (see e.g. Dalton-Puffer 2007) – where thus more often than not CLIL equals CEIL (*content-and-English-integrated learning*) in geography, biology, and many other subjects. The predominance of English as a language for learning also has come to be acknowledged by European institutions themselves. For example, the 2008 edition of the Eurydice network's *Key Data on Teaching Languages at School in Europe* reports that in the vast majority of EU member states over 90 per cent of pupils in secondary schools study English, either as a compulsory subject or as an elective. This tendency is on the rise, and since 2002 the numbers of pupils learning English have been growing especially in the states of Central and Eastern Europe (particularly in Bulgaria, the Czech Republic, Hungary, Slovakia), but also in Portugal. Generally speaking children start learning English at an ever younger age. The Eurydice report summarises the situation thus: "The teaching of English is constantly expanding and predominates almost everywhere" (Eurydice 2008: 12).

The strong presence of English in school curricula is continued in the tertiary sector, where one of the most significant trends is the teaching of courses and degrees exclusively in English (Ammon & McConnel 2002: 171; Truchot 1997: 71; Murray & Dingwall 2001: 86). This process is stimulated (somewhat paradoxically) by policy efforts to create a common European higher education area (cf. The Bologna Process, see http://ec.europa.eu/education/higher-education/doc1290_en.htm), where student and staff mobility result in a strengthening of the most readily available common language.

This trend in tertiary education goes hand in hand with language choice in scientific research, where English is perceived as a sine qua non for accessing information and communicating with fellow academics internationally (Ammon 2001; Viereck 1996). Accordingly, the majority of European scientific associations embrace English as the dominant, or indeed sole, language for the exchange of ideas (Crystal 2003: 88f.). In order to secure an international audience, the use of English in scientific conferences and publications is similarly unquestioned (Ammon 2001: 5; Truchot 2002: 11). As a consequence, scientists seem to "function more as members of an international community having one common language than as members of national communities, both in their writing and in their selection of background readings" (Truchot 1997: 67; see also Widdowson 2003: Chapter 5).

Generally speaking, the situation between Lisbon and Murmansk is that individuals usually have one first language (sometimes more), and are often exposed to other languages spoken locally, but most of them also have contact with English, which can be extensive or minimal – in their professional and private lives. In the early 21st century, the significance of a certain command of English is closely comparable to that of reading and writing at the time of industrialization in Europe (Carmichael 2000: 285f.). Accordingly, proficiency in English is becoming something like a taken-for-granted cultural technique (Grin 1999; Neuner 2002: 7; Breidbach 2003: 20) like literacy or computer skills, with the consequence that on a global scale,

> the competitive advantage which English has historically provided its acquirers (personally, organisationally, and nationally) will ebb away as English becomes a near-universal basic skill.   (Graddol 2006: 15)

This then is the reality of English in Europe. But it is a reality that seems to run counter to the ideal of linguistic diversity that the EU is at pains to promote. English is seen not so much as a means of communal integration but rather as a threat to the status and integrity of other languages. The rhetoric of the protectionism of linguistic diversity persists, ironically enough, even despite the actual practices within the EU itself.

For even though the EU presents itself as an essentially multilingual institution, the supremacy of English is being established step by step in European politics and various European and international organizations in Europe, e.g. the European Commission, the UN or NATO (Dollerup 1996:27pp.). Official multilingual policies are often abandoned in practice in order to facilitate the working process. For example, van Els (2005) reports that all internal and external communication in the European Central Bank (ECB) in Frankfurt is conducted only in English. This restriction to English

> amounts to a tacit agreement within the ECB which everyone adheres to, but it is in no sense a matter of official policy. This characterizes the manner in which the EU deals with the problems of internal communication.   (van Els 2005:269)

There is, then, a marked discrepancy between the European Union's discourse about language and communication on the one hand and the reality on the ground on the other. The forceful and enforced promotion of multilingualism as an official policy is in stark contrast with the actual practice of European citizens and institutions alike increasingly converging towards one lingua franca. How can one account for this discrepancy? Why is there such resistance to openly acknowledging the pragmatic solution that apparently most people are actually subscribing to? Why are official communications and websites suggesting that there is a fully functional multilingualism in EU institutions while unofficially one learns from the people involved that this is simply not the case?

I would suggest that a large part of the explanation for this discrepancy lies in the persistence of a mind-set deeply rooted in history. Europeans tend to carry with them what Florian Coulmas once called "the ideological dead weight of the nineteenth century" (Coulmas 1991:27). This is characterised by a conflating of political loyalties with linguistic loyalties, and of language with culture. The unification and formation of nation states in the 19th century with its close association of nationhood and language still shapes the mindsets of many of today's Europeans. And this sense of independent national lingua-cultural identity has, of course, been strengthened by a long history of conflict and striving for dominance among countries in relatively close geographical proximity. It is no wonder that the question as to 'who has to learn whose language' is inextricably linked in people's minds to issues of power. No wonder either that people should feel so protective of their language as a symbol of separate national and communal identity. Of course linguistic standardization, the status planning of languages, played an important role in confirming this identity. This necessarily involved the reduction of diversity, the giving up of emblems of individual or group identity for the greater good of shared values of the larger linguacultural community and thus the monolingual individual came to be seen as the unmarked case.

The very size and linguacultural heterogeneity of Europe makes this principle of nation building impossible to apply at the supranational EU level.

Instead, what prevails is the sense of the interdependency of language and national identity and with it the conviction that if a language is dominant, the nation that 'owns' it is bound to be dominant, too. Hence the insistence on the (theoretical) equality of all languages in a union where all the member states are claimed to be equal partners. This is an ideology of diversity that overrides the need for greater unity and uniformity in the interests of the larger community. The ideology is apparent in official pronouncements of the kind found, for example, in the EU Commission's *Europa languages portal*:

> Each Member State, when it joins the Union, stipulates which language or languages it wants to have declared official languages of the EU.
>
> So the Union uses the languages chosen by its citizens' own national governments, *not a single language or a few languages chosen by itself and which many people in the Union might not understand*
> [...]
> Our policy of official multilingualism as a deliberate tool of government is unique in the world. The EU sees the use of its citizens' languages as one of the factors which make it more transparent, more legitimate and more efficient. The European Union has recognised the importance of its special language policy by appointing a top official to champion the cause at the highest level. The portfolio of Leonard Orban includes responsibility for multilingualism.
> (http://europa.eu/languages/en/home, accessed 20 /2/2010; emphasis added)[1]

Here it is clear that ideology takes precedence not only over reality but over rationality too. The assumption, in defiance of logic, is that allowing national governments to stipulate their own languages as "official" somehow guarantees that these will be understood by other citizens in the Union. This constitutes a declaration of the EU's commitment to furthering "unity in diversity", a commitment that is to be discharged by "a top official" who is to "champion the cause". Diversity, then, is seen as a cause to be championed and not a case to be argued for.

"Unity in diversity" is, of course, an appealing slogan, but as a realistic proposition it presents formidable challenges, for, as I have already indicated, the present quest for it is beset with the counter influence of past history. Europe is "a

---

1.   In the second Barroso Commission, from early February 2010, the post of Commissioner for Multilingualism ceased to exist and the portfolio was re-merged with that of the Commissioner for Education, Culture, Multilingualism and Youth. The text on the website, however, remained unchanged at least up to the date of access indicated.

continent where the tradition of 'one language, one state, one people' is [...] deeply entrenched" (Wright 2000: 1), where national languages have great symbolic importance, with long traditions and close ties with their speakers' socio-cultural identities. As I have already pointed out, linguistic diversity within the state has in the past been deliberately suppressed by standardization in countries like France in the interests of national unity and socio-cultural cohesion. The independent status of European national languages, often hard won, is therefore highly prized and jealously guarded.

The forceful, and fanciful, rhetoric in support of Europe's multilingual image, in which the notion of linguistic diversity figures like a mantra is, then, at odds with reality. Linguistic diversity appears not to be high on the list of priorities of the citizens themselves, who predominantly go for English if given a choice, plus a few other 'big' languages. This is, of course, unwelcome news to policy makers and when confronted with this reality, they are naturally inclined to explain it away. Here is an example from the Eurydice document Key Data on Teaching Languages at School in Europe:

> The sometimes very broad range of possible foreign languages included in the curricula of several countries (Figure B10) may reflect the determination of educational policy-makers to diversify school provision for foreign language learning. However, statistical data on this provision indicate that in secondary education, English, French, German, Spanish and Russian represent over 95% of all languages learnt in the majority of countries (Figure C9). [...] Pupils thus essentially appear to opt for learning more widely used languages. *This may be attributable either to pressure from families or a lack of qualified teachers in other languages.*   (Eurydice 2008: 11, emphasis added)

The last sentence highlighted above comes across as an attempt to avoid precisely what seems to be at issue here: surely the questions that need to be asked in this context are just why there should be "pressure from families" and "a lack of qualified teachers in other languages". When 90% of learners opt for the most widely used language, English, then exhortations to choose other languages will be to no avail.

The preference for English is, naturally enough, seen as a threat to the maintenance of linguistic diversity. All languages are supposed to be equal but English is obviously 'more equal than the others'. The protection of other languages is therefore assumed to involve resistance to English. To assume this, however, is to think of the language as just like any other, essentially the property of its native speakers, imbued with their culture and expressive of their identity. But English as a lingua franca is not like other European languages for it has been removed from native speaker ownership, appropriated and adapted for international use on a massive and unprecedented scale.

As I have argued in more detail elsewhere (e.g. Seidlhofer, Breiteneder & Pitzl 2006; Seidlhofer 2011), it is this global spread of English as an international lingua franca, as ELF, that calls for its radical reconceptualization. The notion of 'a language' as inextricably tied to its native speakers and indivisible from their culture simply does not apply. What needs to be recognized is that the lingua franca – especially if it is used on a daily basis as is now the case for increasing numbers of Europeans – ceases to be the property of the ancestral speakers in whose territories it originated. Instead, ELF gets appropriated by its non-native users, who then become agents in the processes that determine how the language spreads, develops, varies, and changes (Brumfit 2001; Brutt-Griffler 2002; Widdowson 2003: Chapter 5).

This reconceptualization of English has very considerable implications for European language policy if this policy could be freed from its ideological commitment. One case in point is the perennial problem of the proliferation of official languages and the contested proposals for settling on one, two or three working language(s) – English, plus French, plus German. Van Els (2005) discusses various options that have been suggested and leaves no doubt as to which solution he favours:

> There is a [further] modality that perhaps has a better prospect of success. This one, however, does impose a very drastic restriction, i.e. to only a single working language. It may seem surprising, but in this modality the language handicap for non-natives, as opposed to the variant with a number of working languages, is significantly reduced. In the first place, they only need to develop competence in one foreign language. Secondly, and this is very important, this one foreign language will also become – and to an increasing extent – the property of the non-natives. If they constitute a large majority, as in the EU, they will, without doubt, use the working language as their language and share in the fashioning of this language to meet their own needs. Native speakers will notice – sometimes to their great annoyance – that their language is frequently being changed in unorthodox ways. (van Els 2005: 276)

The one working language van Els is talking about in the above quote is English: "*Without any doubt, English will be the working language*" (op.cit.: 278, original emphasis), and from what the author says about the role of non-native users' share "in the fashioning of this language to meet their own needs" it is clear that by "English" he means ELF.

This is a view shared by Wright (2009). She also presents the case for the acceptability of ELF as the lingua franca of the EU and relates this to what I referred to earlier as the disparity between rhetoric and reality, or what she describes as "the unresolved clash between top-down policy and bottom-up practice, and the unacknowledged language problems this causes in both the European institutions and the wider world" (Wright 2009: 97). She observes:

> At present, the linguistic side effect of current social phenomena is linguistic convergence towards a single lingua franca. Language policy cannot work against these social currents and impose multilingualism from the top down. It alone will not reverse the trend to use English as a lingua franca. If the move to English is halted, it will be because of other, external factors that we cannot yet foresee. We can do little to influence this and the lesson that we should take from the nation-state experience is not that language policy can be imposed from the top down but that this only works when it is in harmony with other social, political and economic developments.
>
> (op.cit.: 107)

What, I have argued, is crucial to the acceptability and functionality of English as the common means of communication is its explicit conceptualisation as ELF rather than the native language of the British and the Irish. This is what van Els is referring to in his proposal, and what Wright emphasises too. Importantly, she makes the key point (entirely missed, one might add, by Phillipson 2003) that whatever validity the argument might have for seeing the predominance of English in terms of Gramscian hegemony, this cannot simply be mapped from colonial situations onto Europe:

> [...] in the European setting, there is no elemental link between centre, power and English. The majority of those in positions of authority using English within elite networks are not native English speakers. They have acquired English as a second language and use it as a lingua franca.   (Wright 2009: 105)

So in Europe today, it is simply not the case that English emanates from the native-speaker 'centre' in a way that is designed to benefit its native speakers. It may be true that these do have some advantage in that they are the only ones that do not need to learn the most widespread European lingua franca from scratch, but it does not follow that they are therefore more adept in its actual communicative use. There are now studies becoming available that show that native speakers of English may actually be at a disadvantage because they tend not to be very effective communicators in intercultural encounters (Jenkins 2007; Wright 2008): "They may not have understood the new rules of engagement, or even grasped that there are such new rules", as Wright (2009: 105) aptly puts it.

It is precisely these rules of engagement that ELF research into intercultural interactions is seeking to achieve a deeper understanding of. Over recent years, an energetic area of enquiry has developed, with corpora of spoken ELF discourse being compiled in order to make detailed descriptions possible. VOICE, the Vienna-Oxford International Corpus of English, comprises data from a range of domains of use, and provides free online access to ELF researchers. ELFA, a corpus of ELF interactions in academic settings, has also been completed.

The insights emerging from empirical studies of naturally-occurring ELF interactions (see, for example, Mauranen and Ranta 2009 and the papers cited at http://www.univie.ac.at/voice/) help us perceive and understand how people from diverse linguacultural backgrounds appropriate and adapt English for their own needs, make it "their English" (see Kohn, this volume). ELF speakers make use of their multi-faceted plurilingual repertoires in ways motivated by the communicative purpose and the interpersonal dynamics of the situation. They draw on the underlying resources of the language, not just the conventional encodings of English as a native language, and adjust and calibrate their own language use for their interlocutors' benefit. Thus they exploit the potential of the language while fully focused on the purpose of the talk and on their interlocutors as people rather than on the linguistic code itself. Now that we are able to investigate naturally-occurring ELF interactions closely, the general picture that is emerging, nearly a decade on from Knapp (2002), is certainly not one of inarticulate, linguistically handicapped non-native speakers incapable of holding their own in interactions with both other non-native as well as native speakers of English, but of an agreed-upon lingua franca employed in a fashion that is appropriate to the occasion – and appropriated, negotiated and shaped by all its users.

These descriptive findings, in turn, bring us back to the theoretical challenges mentioned above since they raise important issues about what 'English' is and how it can be described. They reveal that the widespread assumption that one cannot communicate effectively without adhering to the norms of native English is a myth. So, even at this relatively early stage of analysis, it is evident that ELF users appropriate and exploit linguistic resources in complex and creative ways to achieve their communicative purposes. They use the language at their disposal to negotiate meaning and personal relationships and so co-construct mutual understanding and establish the common conceptual and affective ground of a 'third space'. The very linguistic 'abnormalities' of ELF talk in reference to the norms of native English draw attention to the essentially normal functions they realize as a natural and actually occurring use of language.

What needs to be stressed is that this *natural* English is not the *national* English of its native speakers. It cannot be if it is to serve its essential function as a means for making the concept of unity an operational reality rather than an ideological illusion. As a lingua franca, English is necessarily complementary to other languages in Europe and not in competition with them. And since this is the way

English is used, it would seem to make sense to make provision for this in the way it is conceived of as a subject in educational policy.

It would seem obvious that if educational policy is to take account of reality, English – conceived of as a lingua franca – needs to be taken out of the canon of 'real' foreign languages and recognized as a co-existent and non-competitive addition to the learner/user's linguistic repertoire (Seidlhofer 2003). Thus English is removed from contention with other languages and thereby, far from reducing diversity in language choice in educational institutions, actually enhances it. It is only when English is conceived of as belonging to its native speakers and as a foreign language like any other that it constitutes a threat.

And yet, in the documents put out by the Language Policy Division of the Council of Europe that *is* how English is persistently represented – just like other foreign languages, defined by its native speakers. The focus has so far remained very much on 'cumulative' proficiency (becoming better at speaking and writing English as native speakers do) and on the goal of successful communication with native speakers (and for some levels, approximating native-like command of the language). It is true that a general shift in curricular guidelines has taken place from 'correctness' to 'appropriateness' and 'intelligibility', but by and large 'intelligibility' is taken to mean being intelligible to native speakers, and being able to understand native speakers. This orientation is clearly discernible in some of the specifications of the European Language Portfolio:

> I can interact with a degree of fluency and spontaneity that makes regular interaction with native speakers quite possible. I can take an active part in discussion in familiar contexts, accounting for and sustaining my views. (Spoken Interaction / B2)

> I have no difficulty in understanding any kind of spoken language, whether live or broadcast, even when delivered at fast native speed, provided I have some time to get familiar with the accent. (Listening / C2)
>
> (http://www.coe.int/portfolio, accessed 20/2/2010)

In a similar vein, Hoffman (2000: 19) describes the English of European learners as spanning "the whole range from non-fluent to native-like", as though fluency in English were not a possibility for those whose speech does not mimic that of a native speaker.

In policy statements, curriculum specifications and teaching materials alike, Standard British English or American English norms are taken for granted as the only valid measures of proficiency. The advocacy of 'authentic' materials constitutes a kind of pedagogic mantra, and teachers are expected to help their learners cope with 'real English', which is taken to be the English used by native speakers in their speech communities in e.g. the UK or the US. This 'real

English' can, of course, now be described with unprecedented accuracy due to the availability of huge corpora of native English. The effect of this has been to further consolidate the position of native-speaker English as the only English that counts and in so doing necessarily ensures the continuation of its conflict with other competing languages and provides further confirmation of fears that it will prevail and dominate.

It is understandable that when only descriptions of native speaker English were available these should have served as the sole reference for specifying the language for learning. There was no alternative. But, as I have pointed out earlier, descriptions of ELF are now under way and what they show is that the English of Europe is in reality very different in form and function from the English as conceived by European educational policy. This, at the very least, should lead us to a reconceptualising of English and to the critical questioning of the taken-for-granted assumptions derived from the past that continue to inform EU language and education policies in the present.

References

Ammon, U. (ed.). 2001. *The Dominance of English as a Language of Science. Effects on Other Languages and Language Communities.* Berlin: Mouton de Gruyter.

Ammon, U. & McConnel, G. 2002. *English as an Academic Language in Europe: A Survey of its Use in Teaching.* Frankfurt: Peter Lang.

Berns, M., de Bot, K. & Hasebrink, U. (eds). 2007. *In the Presence of English: The Media and European Youth.* Berlin: Springer.

Breidbach, S. 2003. *Plurilingualism, Democratic Citizenship and the Role of English.* Strasbourg: Language Policy Division, Council of Europe. <http://www.coe.int/t/dg4/linguistic/Source/BreidbachEN.pdf>, (20 February, 2010).

Brumfit, C. J. 2001. *Individual Freedom in Language Teaching: Helping learners to Develop a Dialect of Their Own.* Oxford: OUP.

Brutt-Griffler, J. 2002. *World English. A Study of its Development.* Clevedon: Multilingual Matters.

Carmichael, C. 2000. Conclusions: Language and national identify in Europe. In *Language and Nationalism in Europe*, S. Barbour & C. Carmichael (eds), 280–289. Oxford: OUP.

Coulmas, F. 1991. European integration and the idea of the national language. In *A Language Policy for the European Community. Prospects and Quandaries*, F. Coulmas (ed.), 1–43. Berlin: Mouton de Gruyter.

Crystal, D. 2003. *English as a Global Language*, 2nd edn. Cambridge: CUP.

Dalton-Puffer, C. 2007. *Discourse in CLIL Classrooms* [Language Learning & Language Teaching 20]. Amsterdam: John Benjamins.

Dollerup, C. 1996. English in the European Union. In *The English Language in Europe*, R. Hartmann (ed.), 24–36. Oxford: Intellect Ltd.

Eurydice. 2008. *Key Data on Teaching Languages at School in Europe.* <http://eacea.ec.europa. eu/education/eurydice/documents/key_data_series/095EN.pdf>, (20 February, 2010).

Graddol, D. 2006. *English Next: Why Global English May Mean the End of 'English as a Foreign Language'.* London: British Council.

Grin, F. 1999. Market forces, language spread and linguistic diversity. In *Language – A Right and a Resource,* M. Kontra, R. Phillipson, T. Skutnabb-Kangas & T. Varady (eds), 169–186. Budapest: Central European University Press.

Hoffman, C. 2000. The spread of English and the growth of multilingualism with English in Europe. In *English in Europe: The Acquisition of a Third Language,* J. Cenoz & U. Jessner (eds), 1–21. Clevedon: Multilingual Matters.

Jenkins, J. 2007. *English as a Lingua Franca: Attitude and Identity.* Oxford: OUP.

Knapp, K. 1987. English as an international lingua franca and the teaching of intercultural communication. In *Perspectives on Language in Performance*: *Studies in Linguistics, Literary Criticism and Language Teaching and Learning; To Honour Werner Hüllen on the Occasion of His Sixtieth Birthday,* W. Lörscher & R. Schulze (eds), 1022–1039. Tübingen: Narr.

Knapp, K. 2002. The fading out of the non-native speaker: Native dominance in lingua-franca-situations. In *Lingua Franca Communication,* K. Knapp & C. Meierkord (eds), 217–244. Frankfurt: Peter Lang.

Labrie, N. & Quell, C. 1997. Your language, my language or English? The potential language choice in communication among nationals of the European Union. *World Englishes* 16: 3–26.

Mauranen, A. & Ranta, E. (eds). 2009. *English as a Lingua Franca: Studies and Findings.* Newcastle-upon-Tyne: Cambridge Scholars Publishing.

Melchers, G. & Shaw, P. 2003. *World Englishes.* London: Arnold.

Murray, H. & Dingwall, S. 2001. The dominance of English at European universities: Switzerland and Sweden compared. In *The Dominance of English as a Language of Science. Effects on Other Languages and Language Communities,* U. Ammon (ed.), 85–112. Berlin: Mouton de Gruyter.

Neuner, G. 2002. *Policy approaches to English.* Strasbourg: Language Policy Division, Council of Europe. <http://www.coe.int/t/dg4/linguistic/Source/NeunerEN.pdf> (20 February, 2010).

Pennycook, A. 2007. *Global Englishes and Transcultural Flows.* London: Routledge.

Phillipson, R. 2003. *English-Only Europe?* London: Routledge.

Preisler, B. 1999. Functions and forms of English in a European ELF country. In *Standard English. The Widening Debate,* T. Bex & R. J. Watts (eds), 239–267. London: Routledge.

Seidlhofer, B. 2003. *A concept of 'international English' and related issues: From 'real English' to 'realistic English'?* Strasbourg: Council of Europe. <http://www.coe.int/t/dg4/linguistic/ Source/SeidlhoferEN.pdf>, (20 February, 2010).

Seidlhofer, B. 2011. *Understanding English as a Lingua Franca.* Oxford: OUP.

Seidlhofer, B., Breiteneder, A. & Pitzl, M.-L. 2006. English as a lingua franca in Europe: challenges for applied linguistics. *Annual Review of Applied Linguistics* 26: 1–34.

Truchot, C. 1997. The spread of English: From France to a more general perspective. *World Englishes* 16: 65–76.

Truchot, C. 2002. *Key Aspects of the Use of English in Europe.* Strasbourg: Language Policy Division, Council of Europe. <http://www.coe.int/t/dg4/linguistic/Source/TruchotEN.pdf>, (20 February, 2010).

Truchot, C. 2003. Some facts and some questions on the use of English in the workplace. In *Europäische Sprachenpolitik. European language policy,* R. Ahrens (ed.), 303–310. Heidelberg: Universitätsverlag Winter.

van Els, T. 2005. Multilingualism in the European Union. *International Journal of Applied Linguistics* 15(3): 263–281.

Viereck, W. 1996. English in Europe: Its nativisation and use as a lingua franca, with special reference to German-speaking countries. In *The English Language in Europe,* R. Hartmann (ed.), 16–23. Oxford: Intellect Ltd.

Widdowson, H. G. 2003. *Defining Issues in English Language Teaching.* Oxford: OUP.

Wright, S. 2000. *Community and Communication. The Role of Language in Nation State Building and European Integration.* Clevedon: Multilingual Matters.

Wright, S. 2008. The case of the crucial and problematic lingua franca. Presentation, AILA 2008: The 15th World Congress of Applied Linguistics, Essen, Germany, August 24–29.

Wright, S. 2009. The elephant in the room. *European Journal of Language Policy* 1(2): 93–120.

Corpora

ELFA: <http://www.uta.fi/laitokset/kielet/engf/research/elfa/corpus.htm>.
VOICE: <http://www.univie.ac.at/voice/>.

English as a foreign language

The role of out-of-school language input

Marjolijn H. Verspoor, Kees de Bot and Eva van Rein
University of Groningen, the Netherlands

This chapter investigates to what extent the process of second language acquisition is influenced by amount and type of input. After a brief description of the place of English in the lives of secondary school students in the Netherlands, the article reports on a semi-longitudinal study comparing students whose out-of-school contact with English is quite limited and a group of students who have regular access to English popular media. Both groups were tested in a high-input condition (bilingual education) and in a low-input condition (monolingual education). The findings show a complex relation between the role of out-of-school and in-school input and developing proficiency that can only be discovered through a semi-longitudinal approach.

English in the Netherlands

Although Dutch tradesmen have been sailing the world for centuries and have had contact with other languages and cultures since the middle ages, education in foreign languages in the Netherlands only started by the end of the eighteenth and the beginning of the nineteenth century (Wilhelm 1997). Due to the fact that foreign language skills were not considered to be basic requirements for all citizens, language education was restricted to the school types attended by the higher ranks of society that prepared for university entrance. In the mid 19th century, foreign language teaching was still not mandatory for lower level education, but it was basically tolerated. In secondary education French, and to a lesser extent German, dominated the scene, while English was still fairly marginal.

In the late 19th century, however, foreign languages became compulsory subjects at all levels of post primary education. Much later, during the second half of the 20th century, English established itself as the first foreign language in the Dutch educational system. In 1986 it was introduced as a compulsory subject in the last two years of primary education, and a few years later it became the only compulsory language for all types of secondary education, including vocational training. This means that the part of the population that went to school from the late 1970s onwards has had English as a school subject for at least 4 years. Apart from the odd case, it is therefore virtually impossible in the Netherlands to find a purely monolingual speaker of Dutch under the age of 50.

English in the Dutch Educational system

In a comparative study of language education in 35 countries from different parts of the world, Blondin, Edelenbos, Johnstone, Kubanek-German and Taeschner (1998) mention that English teaching in the Netherlands generally starts at age 10 and lasts about 8 years on average. An estimated 92% of all pupils follow English lessons with an average number of 150 minutes a week. English is a compulsory subject in the last two years of primary education (when children are normally 10–12 years old), and by the end of primary education pupils will have received about 50 hours of instruction in English.

With respect to the effectiveness of English in primary education in the Netherlands, Edelenbos, Van der Schoot and Verstralen (2000) report on a study in which levels of proficiency in English were measured in two groups: one with 2 years of experience in primary education and one without English education at primary school. After three months in secondary school, the pupils who had had English at the primary level outperformed the other group, but after eight months this difference had disappeared. This suggests that the advantage of having English in primary education is not utilized in subsequent educational trajectories.

Following European language policy recommendations, a rapidly growing number of primary schools have in recent years started offering foreign languages, particularly English, from the first year of school. The aim is to have more pupils reach high levels of proficiency and a good pronunciation by giving them an early start. When these programmes started there was some worry that an early start may lead to delays in the development of the first language (L1) and that adding another language might be a problem for pupils who enter the educational system with another language than Dutch as their L1. Evaluations have shown that so far these worries are unwarranted and that both English and Dutch develop well in this system (Goorhuis-Brouwer & de Bot 2010). Still, most students enter high school with a low level of English proficiency.

In different types of secondary education, which starts when children are around 12 years of age, English is taught from two to four hours a week from the first year onwards. After four years of vocational training, students should have reached the A2 proficiency level as specified through the Common European

Framework of Reference (CEFR; Council of Europe 2001). For schools offering access to university, students should have reached the B2 level after 6 years.

Several studies in recent years have looked at the implementation of English teaching programmes in schools (Bonnet 2004; Elsen 2009). The general picture is that English language teaching is largely traditional, with very limited use of computer based instruction. The textbook is the most important factor in teaching, which is very much geared towards the requirements of the final examinations. An additional problem is that, partly due to the growth of early English teaching in primary schools, pupils enter with a wide range of proficiencies. Since there is no standard for entrance to secondary school for English, teachers have to deal with these varying levels of proficiency by providing more differentiated teaching, but the transition problem between different levels in the educational system remains to be solved.

Bilingual education and bilingual streams

Somewhat disappointed with the traditional methods of teaching foreign languages, a 'grass-roots' movement in the early 1970's, which included a number of highly motivated teachers and parents, convinced their schools to start a new line of teaching: bilingual education. Bilingual education is commonly regarded as one of the possible means for increasing the efficiency of foreign language teaching in the Dutch secondary school system. In bilingual education, a foreign language (almost exclusively English) is used as the language of instruction for at least half of the school subjects. In the first three years at least 50% of the classes are taught in English, and readings and books for these subjects are in English. Teachers in these programmes need to have at least a B2 level according to the CEFR classification and schools are encouraged to hire native speakers to teach part of the program. International exchanges and e-mail projects are part of the focus on internationalization in these schools.

Bilingual schools are rather selective and require a high score on a test which is taken at the end of primary education (the 'CITO' score, see below). The goal of these bilingual programmes is for the pupils to reach high levels of language proficiency in English. Research by Huibregtse (2001) has shown that this bilingual approach leads to the expected higher levels of proficiency in English without detrimental effect on the pupils' language proficiency in their mother tongue and their achievements in school subjects. At the time of writing (2009) there were more than 100 schools offering a bilingual (i.e., Dutch/English) programme (Europees Platform 2008). This goes to show that this approach to English education is attractive to many pupils and schools.

Other sources of English acquisition

While school remains an important source for the acquisition of any foreign language, other sources are becoming more and more important. Research focussing on the use of English media by Dutch (secondary) school pupils shows that lyrics of popular songs, video games and programmes and movies in English contribute significantly to the total input of English (Bonnet 2004; Berns, de Bot & Hasebrink 2007).

The CBS (Dutch Central Bureau of Statistics) 2002 yearbook presents statistics on the way young people tend to spend their leisure time. All age groups (from age 6 onwards) watched television for an average of 163 minutes daily in 1999 and 2000. In the group of 12 to17 years, an average of 165 minutes per day was spent on TV/video/radio. Bonnet (2004) presents data showing that pupils spend some three hours a day listening to English music and watch English programmes on TV for another three hours.

One of the reasons that English is so popular and widespread in the Netherlands (as well as in the Nordic countries of Western Europe and the Dutch-speaking part of Belgium) is that television programmes are not dubbed but instead subtitled. This means that television constitutes an important source of contact with foreign languages. Informal counting shows that 40 to 60% of the programmes on Dutch speaking television channels are actually in a foreign language, mainly English. In addition to popular English speaking television channels like MTV and Discovery Channel, this means that on average, Dutch television viewers will get at least one hour of English input every day. Earlier research (de Bot, Jagt, Janssen, Kessels & Schils 1986) has shown that watching subtitled TV programmes does not mean that only the subtitles are attended to: information is drawn both from the spoken language and from the subtitles. Research by the Dutch broadcasting association (NOS 1977) shows that the Dutch population clearly prefers subtitling over dubbing. Keeping up or developing foreign language skills is mentioned as one of the motives.

A related source of English for Dutch pupils is advertising. English is very noticeably present in various forms of advertising in the Netherlands. This domain seems to be at the forefront in the spread of English. Gerritsen, van Meurs and Gijsbers (2000) made an inventory of television commercials in which English is used. The data show that about a third of the commercials were partly or completely in English.

In debates on the effectiveness of foreign language teaching in different countries (see, e.g., the special issue of The Modern Language Journal 91, 2007), the English media input in the Netherlands, Belgium, and the Nordic countries is often mentioned as the main reason for their effective programmes. However, so far it has been difficult, if not impossible, to assess the relative contribution of different types of input on language acquisition because most pupils get more or less the same amount and type of input, and attempts to relate differences in proficiency to differences in input have not been successful, probably due to these small differences. Kuppens (2007), however, presents data from Flanders, the Dutch-speaking part of Belgium, which show that watching subtitled English programmes had a positive effect on English vocabulary development in secondary school pupils, while no effects were found for listening to songs in English or playing English videogames.

There is, however, a small group of pupils in the Dutch educational system that is exposed to very little English outside the school for religious reasons. Some Dutch Reformed groups that have set up their own denominational schools do not allow their members to listen to popular radio or to watch television. Also the use of the Internet is limited. Pupils from these groups are interesting to study in that they may help us determine the role of input in English outside school. Henceforth, we will refer to them as 'non-media' students, groups or pupils.

On the whole, these non-media students follow the same educational path as other Dutch pupils, with equal numbers of hours of English in the curriculum, but they enter secondary school without having been in contact with English through the popular media. During their school career their out-of-school input from English is thus very limited compared to that of pupils in other schools. Because students from the Reformed schools were traditionally scoring much lower on English as a subject in the Dutch final exams, several Reformed schools have started bilingual programmes to try and compensate for their lack of input.

In this contribution, we report on a comparative study of pupils in these Reformed schools (i.e., the 'non-media' group) and in non-denominational schools, (the 'media' group), either in monolingual or bilingual programmes. Four groups of pupils have been included in the project: Monolingual Non-media (Mo/Non-Media), Bilingual Education Non-media (Bi/NonMedia), Monolingual Media (Mo/Media), and Bilingual Media (Bi/Media). The aim is to see to what extent the Mo/NonMedia group differs from its Mo/Media counterpart and to what extent the Bi/NonMedia group is able to compensate for the lack of media input.

Description of the research project

Schools

We present data from one Reformed school and three other schools. All four schools have both a bilingual and a monolingual programme. The data are part of

Table 1. Number of pupils in each category: First grade of secondary school

Year 1	Media	Non-Media
Bilingual	83	26
Monolingual	104	27

Table 2. Number of pupils in each category: Third grade of secondary school

Year 3	Media	Non-Media
Bilingual	74	27
Monolingual	184	31

a larger project aimed at the assessment of the effectiveness of bilingual education as a follow-up to the Huibregtse (2001) study mentioned earlier. The Reformed school is in a rural environment in what is considered part of the 'Bible Belt', an area in the Netherlands where traditional Protestantism is prevalent. The other three schools (i.e. the media monolingual and bilingual schools) are located in towns in the middle of the Netherlands; one media bilingual school is located in the western part of the Netherlands. In all bilingual schools the bilingual track is a highly selective track for more talented students, and such schools always have a regular monolingual track.

Data reported on here are from the pupils in the first and third year of secondary school (ages 13 and 15). For an overview of the number of students in each category, see Tables 1 and 2.

At the beginning of the study, a questionnaire asking for background information and containing can-do statements was administered in Dutch. All first-year students were also given an English reading test to assess their entrance level reading proficiency at the beginning of their high school education. At the beginning and twice more during the year, two English proficiency tests were given: a vocabulary test and a writing task. All questionnaires and tests were computer-based and administered at each school's computer laboratory under supervision of the English teacher. There was no time pressure for any of the tests. The students were informed that the outcomes of the test would not influence their normal grades.

Instruments used at the beginning of the school year
Cito scores. To assess differences in scholastic aptitude, we made use of CITO (Centraal Instituut voor Toetsontwikkeling/Dutch Testing Institute) scores. Most pupils in the Dutch educational system take this test at the end of primary school. Their CITO scores, in addition to recommendations by school principals, determine what type of high school pupils can go to. The groups we looked at are all

in the highest academic ranges with scores larger than 535, out of a maximum of 550. Within schools only the very brightest (usually a CITO score higher than 545) are allowed in the bilingual programme, so we expect differences between the monolingual and bilingual students' Cito scores since students who score lower than 535 are not admitted to the bilingual programmes.

Background questionnaire. To assess the amount of contact learners had with English and in order to find out how often they used English, we used a questionnaire developed by Berns et al. (2007). The questionnaire also contained questions pertaining to motivation and attitudes towards English and other background information.

Self-assessment of English proficiency. To determine the way students assess themselves on English proficiency, a self-assessment test using a number of statements pertaining to the can-do scales from the CEFR set (such as: I can read a normal newspaper in English/I can understand a basic news programme in English) was administered in Dutch. The statements used refer to language use ranging between the CEFR levels of A1 and B1.

A reading test. For the first-year students a standardized English reading test for elementary school was used to assess proficiency levels at the start of secondary school.

Instruments used both at the beginning of the year and twice more during the year
Vocabulary test. Students were tested on their passive vocabulary knowledge by means of the EFL (English as a Foreign Language) test (this is a yes/no test developed by Meara & Buxton 1987), which contained words in different frequency ranges. Students were asked to indicate whether they did or did not know the words. The test also contains a number of pseudo-words. The first-year pupils were tested on the most frequent words. A 1000–2000 word level test (120 words in each test) was used three times in all. For the third-year pupils a 3000–4000 word level test (120 words) was used for the first two testing times. A longer test (180 words) using a 3000–5000 word level was used the third time. Scores on the EFL-test were calculated to compensate for 'guessers' by way of the I_{sdt} scoring method developed by Huibregtse, Admiraal and Meara (2002). This means that the scores for this vocabulary test can be anywhere between 0 and 1. Higher scores reflect higher vocabulary knowledge.

Writing task. Various written tasks were performed as well. All assignments were on personal topics and increased in difficulty over the years, but they were also

Table 3. Writing assignments used in the study

Time	Year	Assignment
October 2007	1	Write a short story (± 150 words) about your new school, friends and teachers.
October 2007	3	Write a short story (± 150 words) about the most awful (or best) thing that happened to you during summer vacation. It does not have to be truthful.
February 2008	1	Pretend you have a foreign penpal. Tell him/her about your favourite holiday and explain what you find so special about it. (± 150 words)
February 2008	3	Pretend you have just won 1,000 euros. Write a short story (± 150 words) about what you would do with the money.
June 2008	1	Write about the most awful (or best) thing that happened to you at school so far. It does not have to be truthful. (± 150 words)
June 2008	3	Pretend your school principal has stated that from now on anyone should wear a school uniform. Write him/her a short letter (± 150 words) to explain why you agree/do not agree with this new rule.

easy enough for the less proficient students. Table 3 shows the writing assignments given throughout the year. There was no time limit, but there was a 150-
word limit per assignment because of the computer software used.

A holistic score was given to each text by a team of 8 experienced EFL teachers. To ensure inter-rater reliability, a thorough assessment procedure was conducted. The group of eight raters first evaluated six essays individually in order to
determine which ones were the strongest and which ones the weakest. Then the
group of raters discussed each set of six until consensus was reached. Discussions
amongst the raters established a range of factors that seemed to play a role in
determining proficiency: vocabulary range, sentence complexity, use of L1, use of
tenses, use of authentic expressions, accuracy, etc. When agreement was reached
on the rank order, the texts were tentatively classified into seven proficiency levels
(0–7). Following this procedure, the raters worked together with about 100 essays
until they settled on these proficiency levels. Assessment criteria were then established which included the main characteristics of each level that had emerged
to help the raters classify the remainder of the essays. Afterwards, the group of
raters divided into two groups of four and assessed the samples per page (first
individually) and then compared the scores. The score of the majority (3 out of 4)
was taken and differences in opinion were resolved in discussion. If a group was
unable to reach consensus, the other group of raters was consulted.

Design
This is a semi-longitudinal, cross-sectional study. Both first and third year students were tested on proficiency three times a year.

Table 4. First year students: Scores for the CITO, reading test, self-assessment and motivation/attitudes

	CITO scores		Reading scores		Self-assessment		Motivation/attitude	
	M	sd	M	sd	M	sd	M	sd
Bi/NonMedia	547	2.63	6.9	1.88	2.8	0.11	3.1	0.40
Mo/NonMedia	545	3.13	5.6	2.13	2.6	0.10	2.8	0.32
Bi/Media	547	3.53	7.8	1.72	3.2	0.05	3.2	0.33
Mo/Media	544	3.82	6.1	2.34	2.9	0.05	3.0	0.44

Results for the background information
First year students. In order to assess whether the out-of-school input had an impact on the development of proficiency, we had to control for the other variables, viz., scholastic aptitude, reading proficiency, self-assessment, and motivation/attitude. Table 4 presents the data for the CITO scores, the reading scores, and the self-assessment and motivation/attitude scores for the four groups in their first year of high school. Univariate tests were performed to see if there were any general differences between groups and post-hoc tests to compare the groups more specifically (either Gabriel's if Levene's test showed that variances were equal or Games-Howell's in those cases were variances were not equal; the alpha level was set at $p < .05$).

There was a significant difference between groups for the Cito scores ($F (3, 208) = 9.067, p < .001, partial\ \eta^2 = .116$). Post-tests show that the Mo/Media students in grade 1 had a significantly lower average Cito-score than either the Bi/Media group ($p < .001$) or the Bi/NonMedia group ($p < .001$).

Groups also differed significantly on the variable reading scores, ($F (3, 146) = 9.365, p < .001, partial\ \eta^2 = .161$). There were no significant differences in reading scores between the two monolingual groups or between the two bilingual groups. However, the Bi/Media group had a significantly higher score than either the Mo/Media group ($p < .001$) or the Mo/NonMedia group ($p < .001$).

In self-assessment we also see some differences ($F (3, 182) = 11.392, p < .001, partial\ \eta^2 = .158$). The Mo/NonMedia students rated themselves significantly lower than the Mo/Media group ($p < .05$). The Bi/Media students rated their English proficiency higher than both the Mo/Media ($p < .01$) and the Mo/NonMedia group ($p < .001$), and also higher than the Bi/NonMedia group ($p < .01$). There were no further differences in self-assessment.

As far as motivation/attitudes was concerned, the difference between groups was significant at $F (3, 3210) = 7.304, p < .001, partial\ \eta^2 = .094$. The Mo/NonMedia group had a significantly lower score than the Mo/Media group ($p < .05$).

Table 5. The correlations between self-assessment, reading and motivation in the first year students

	Reading	Self-assessment	Motivation
Reading	1	0.366 (**)	0.196 (*)
Self-assessment	0.366 (**)	1	0.357 (**)
Motivation	0.196 (*)	0.357 (**)	1

** significant at the 0.01 level
* significant at the 0.05 level

There was also a significant difference between the Bi/NonMedia group and the Mo/NonMedia group ($p < .05$) and a significant difference between the Bi/Media group and both the Mo/Media ($p < .05$) and the Mo/NonMedia group ($p < .001$).

It is interesting to note that self-assessment correlated moderately with both the reading test and motivation, suggesting that the self-assessment scores reflected some of the variation in proficiency (Table 5).

To summarize, when they entered high school, the two monolingual groups (Mo/NonMedia and Mo/Media) were rather similar in scholastic aptitude and reading score. There was a significant difference in self-assessment and in motivation/attitude. The two bilingual groups (Bi/NonMedia-Bi/Media) were also rather similar in scholastic aptitude, reading score, and motivation. There was, however, a significant difference in self-assessment.

Third year students. For the third year students, the same instruments were used for background information as for the first year students. However, no reading test was administered as it was too easy for these students. Table 6 presents the scores for the third year students.

There were no significant differences between the two monolingual groups or between the two bilingual groups as far as the Cito scores were concerned. However, as anticipated, the monolingual groups showed a significantly lower score than the bilinguals ($F (3, 192) = 7.205, p < .001, partial \eta^2 = .101$). The Mo/NonMedia group scored lower than the Bi/NonMedia group ($p < .01$) or the Bi/Media group ($p < .05$), and the Mo/Media group scored significantly lower than the Bi/Media group ($p < .01$) or the Bi/NonMedia group ($p < .01$). Note that the means were the same as for the first year students.

For self-assessment there were significant differences ($F (3, 178 = 18.635, p < .001, partial \eta^2 = .239$). The Mo/NonMedia group scored significantly lower than the Mo/Media group ($p < .01$). The Bi/NonMedia group scored significantly lower than the Bi/Media group ($p < .001$). The Bi/Media students also had a significantly higher score than the Mo/Media ($p < .001$) and the Mo/NonMedia group ($p < .001$).

Table 6. Third year students: Scores for the CITO test, self-assessment and motivation/attitudes

	CITO scores		Self-assessment		Motivation/attitude	
	M	sd	M	sd	M	sd
Bi/NonMedia	547	2.48	3.2	0.25	2.9	0.40
Mo/NonMedia	544	4.22	2.9	0.55	2.9	0.44
Bi/Media	547	3.13	3.6	0.35	3.2	0.31
Mo/Media	545	3.90	3.3	0.48	3.1	0.45

The difference between groups for motivation was also significant (F (3, 199) = 7.682, $p < .001$, *partial η^2* = .104). There was no difference between the two monolingual groups for motivation, but there was a significant difference between the two bilingual groups. The Bi/Media students had a significantly higher score than the Bi/NonMedia group ($p < .001$). The Bi/Media students also scored significantly higher than the Mo/Media ($p < .05$) and the Mo/NonMedia group ($p < .001$). There also was a significant correlation between self-assessment and motivation in year three (r = 0.464, $p < .01$) .

To summarize, at the beginning of their third year in high school, some differences between the groups can be seen (see also Table 6). The monolingual groups were similar to each other in scholastic aptitude and motivation/attitude, but differed significantly in self-assessment. The bilingual groups were similar to each other in scholastic aptitude, and also differed from each other in self-assessment. Unlike the first-year groups, they also differed in motivation/attitude.

Out-of-school input English

The questionnaire on out-of-school input contained a long list of potential sources related to family and friends, books, and so on. Table 7 shows the results of a standard factor analysis. The factors that correlated highly with each other are printed in bold. The factor analysis led to a three factor solution suggesting three kinds of input: (1) popular media (movies, music), (2) traditional media (books, talk on radio) and (3) personal contact.

The statistical analyses (see Table 8) of the scores for degrees of contact (1 is low and 4 is high) show that there were significant differences between groups (F (3, 410) = 21.719, $p < .001$, *partial η^2* = .137). Post-tests confirmed our hypothesis that the non-media groups had significantly less out-of-school contact with English than their media counterparts (the Bi/NonMedia scores were significantly lower than the Bi/Media scores ($p < .001$)). Similarly, the Mo/NonMedia scores were significantly lower than the Mo/Media scores ($p < .001$). When we look at the three factors individually, though, there was only a significant difference

Table 7. Three factor solution for out-of-school English input. Loadings larger than .5 are presented in italics

	Factor 1 Popular media	Factor 2 Traditional media	Factor 3 Personal contact
Parents/caretakers	−.031	.097	*.794*
Siblings	−.003	.218	*.758*
Friends	.183	.278	*.630*
Music on the radio	*.742*	.115	.046
Speech on the radio	.190	*.621*	.188
Television	*.821*	−.025	.123
Cd's/mp3's	*.827*	.084	.043
Cinema	*.801*	.092	−.078
Newspapers	−.265	*.809*	.096
Magazines	.154	*.782*	.123
Books	.128	*.558*	.237
PC	.351	.341	.209

Table 8. Average scores (1 is low; 4 is high) of out-of school input for first and third year students combined

	Out-of-school contact		Popular media		Traditional media		Personal contact	
	M	Sd	M	Sd	M	Sd	M	Sd
Bi/NonMedia	1.99	0.480	2.06	0.738	1.83	0.637	2.08	0.567
Mo/NonMedia	2.08	0.568	2.37	0.789	1.77	0.609	1.98	0.725
Bi/Media	2.47	0.371	3.24	0.499	1.82	0.487	2.06	0.632
Mo/Media	2.43	0.457	3.22	0.550	1.79	0.568	1.97	0.747

between groups for 'popular media' ($F\,(3,\,419) = 73.914$, $p < .001$), *partial η^2 =* .346). The Bi/NonMedia scores here were significantly lower than the Bi/Media scores ($p < .001$), and the Mo/NonMedia scores were significantly lower than the Mo/Media scores ($p < .001$).

Results proficiency development

First year students. As mentioned earlier, language proficiency was tested by means of a vocabulary test and a writing task three times during the year of data collection. Data on the vocabulary test in all groups are presented in Figure 1.

At the beginning of the first year, there were no significant differences between groups. Differences started to emerge at the second test ($F\,(3,\,187) = 5.092$, $p < .01$, *partial η^2* = .076) and became even more pronounced at the end of the first year ($F\,(3,\,165) = 11.041$, $p < .001$, *partial η^2* = .167).

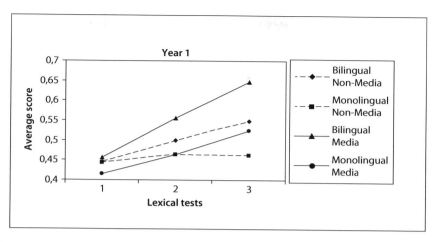

Figure 1. Lexical test data for first year students

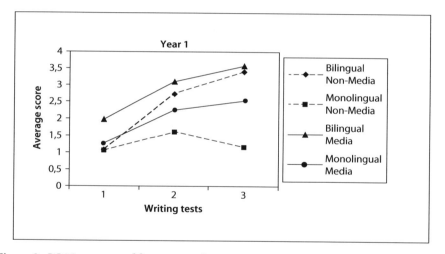

Figure 2. Writing scores of first year students

Throughout the first year, there were no significant differences between the two monolingual groups. The bilingual groups appeared to score higher than the monolingual groups throughout the entire first year, and the media groups appeared to perform better than their non-media peers. However, these differences were only significant when the Bi/Media group were compared to the other groups: this group scored significantly higher on the second test than the Mo/Media group ($p < .01$). The Bi/Media group outperformed all other groups on the last test, including the Bi/NonMedia group ($p < .01$), and the Bi/NonMedia group scored significantly higher than the Mo/NonMedia group ($p < .05$).

There were significant differences between groups at all three writing tests in the first year. At the beginning of the first year ($F (3, 192) = 14.664, p < .001$, partial $\eta^2 = .186$), there were no significant differences between the two monolingual groups, but there was a significant difference between the two bilingual groups. The Bi/Media group performed significantly better on the first test than all other groups, including the Bi/NonMedia group ($p < .001$).

Differences continued to exist for the second test ($F (3, 189) = 21.950, p < .001$, partial $\eta^2 = .258$) and the third test ($F (3, 171) = 52.118, p < .001$, partial $\eta^2 = .478$). The Mo/NonMedia group scored significantly lower than the Mo/Media group on the second test ($p < .01$). There was no significant difference between the two bilingual groups. However, the Bi/Media scores were significantly higher than the Mo/Media and Mo/NonMedia scores ($p < .001$).

On the third writing test, the Mo/NonMedia group again scored significantly lower than the Mo/Media group ($p < .001$). There were no differences between the bilingual groups, but in all relevant cases the bilingual group scores were significantly higher than those of the monolingual groups ($p < .001$).

Third year students. In the third year, similar tests were used as in the first year, but they were more difficult. Like for the first year students, a vocabulary test and a writing task were administered three times during the year of data collection. Figure 3 presents the lexical data for the four groups on the third year tests.

In the third year, groups differed significantly on all three tests: the first test ($F (3, 181) = 32.278, p < .001$, partial $\eta^2 = .349$), the second test ($F (3, 187) = 24.756, p < .001$, partial $\eta^2 = .284$) and the third test ($F (3, 176) = 39.669, p < .001$, partial $\eta^2 = .403$).

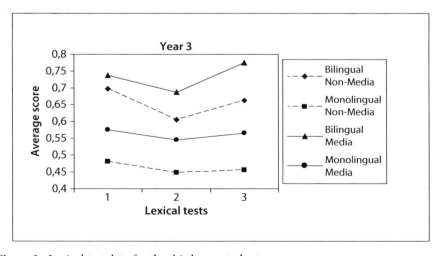

Figure 3. Lexical test data for the third year students

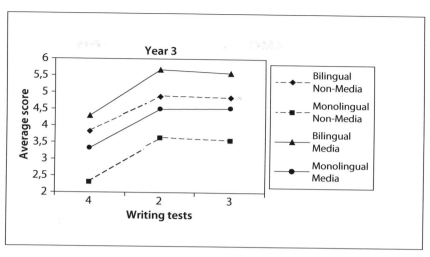

Figure 4. Writing scores for third year students

The Mo/NonMedia group scored significantly lower than the Mo/Media group on all three tests ($p < .01$ in all cases). The Bi/NonMedia group also scored significantly lower than the Bi/Media group on the third test ($p < .01$). The Bi/NonMedia group scored significantly higher than the Mo/NonMedia group on all three tests ($p < .001$ in all cases) and higher than Mo/Media on the first test only ($p < .001$). The Bi/Media group scored significantly higher than the Mo/Media group on all three tests ($p < .001$ in all three cases).

The third year students were also tested three times for writing. Figure 4 presents the data for the four groups.

For writing, groups also differed significantly on all three tests in the third year: the first test ($F(3, 182) = 29.280$, $p < .001$, *partial* $\eta^2 = .326$), the second test ($F(3, 189) = 38.604$, $p < .001$, *partial* $\eta^2 = .380$) and the third test ($F(3, 178) = 34.154$, $p < .001$, *partial* $\eta^2 = .365$).

Again, the Mo/NonMedia group scored significantly lower than the Mo/Media group on all three tests ($p < .001$ in all cases). The Bi/NonMedia group scored significantly lower than the Bi/Media group on the second ($p < .001$) and third tests ($p < .01$). The Mo/NonMedia group also scored significantly lower than the Bi/NonMedia group on all three tests ($p < .001$). The Mo/Media group scored significantly lower than the Bi/Media group throughout the entire year ($p < .001$).

Finally, we explored to what extent in both the first and the third year the amount of input from modern media correlated with the proficiency scores. We expected the correlations to become stronger over time because of a dynamic interaction: the idea is that the more proficient learners are, the more they might listen to texts of songs and movies, enabling them to benefit even more from

Table 9. Correlations between input from popular media and proficiency as measured by a vocabulary test (Voc) and a writing test (Wr) for the first year students

Year 1	Time 1		Time 2		Time 3	
	Voc	Wr	Voc	Wr	Voc	Wr
Popular Media: Monolinguals	−0.002	0.277**	0.067	0.237*	0.097	0.409**
Popular Media: Bilinguals	0.110	0.347**	0.201	0.213*	0.238*	0.225*

** significant at the 0.01 level
* significant at the .05 level

Table 10. Correlations between input from popular media and proficiency as measured by a vocabulary test (Voc) and a writing test (Wr) for the third year students

Year 3	Time 1		Time 2		Time 3	
	Voc	Wr	Voc	Wr	Voc	Wr
Popular Media: Monolinguals	0.160	0.360**	0.305**	0.356**	0.251*	0.360**
Popular Media: Bilinguals	0.348**	0.184	0.335**	0.481**	0.478**	0.378**

** significant at the 0.01 level
* significant at the .05 level

the input. Table 9 shows that in the first year, the monolingual learners showed stronger correlations at the end of the year for writing only. In other words, their productive skills significantly correlated with the amount of popular media input they were receiving. For the bilinguals, this effect was the opposite. Popular media input correlated more strongly with proficiency at the beginning of the year than at the end.

When we look at the third year (see Table 10), the correlations between popular media input and proficiency remained significant. Not only productive skills but also lexical skills (vocabulary) were affected from Time 2 onwards.

To summarize, in the third year the monolingual non-media groups performed significantly lower on all the proficiency tests than their media counterparts. The bilingual non-media groups scored as well as the media monolingual groups but not as well as their bilingual counterparts (this was true for the third lexical test and for the second and third writing tests). The correlations between Popular Media and proficiency scores showed that the interaction of Popular Media with proficiency changed over time. First the productive skills (writing) showed strong correlations. It wasn't until the third year that the receptive skills (vocabulary) showed a significant correlation.

Discussion

In this contribution, we reported on a comparative study of non-media and media pupils in both monolingual and bilingual school programmes. We compared the following groups: Monolingual Non-media (Mo/NonMedia) versus Monolingual Media (Mo/Media) and Bilingual Programme Non-media (Bi/NonMedia), versus Bilingual Media (Bi/Media). The aim was to see to what extent the Mo/NonMedia group differed from its Mo/Media counterparts and to what extent the Bi/Non-Media group was able to compensate for the lack of media input. How did they compare to the Mo/Media and Bi/Media groups?

Our expectation that the non-media groups had less media input than their media peers was confirmed. The non-media pupils had significantly less 'popular' media input. When the non-media students first entered high school, though, none of their objective scores (except for writing for the bilingual group) were significantly lower than those of their media peers. The asterisks in Table 11 show where and when the monolingual and bilingual non-media groups differed significantly from their respective media counterparts.

Our main finding is that the lack of input from the media had a long term effect on the developing proficiencies of the non-media group as English language

Table 11. Summary of differences amongst the two monolingual groups and the two bilingual groups

	Measures at starting point	Time 1	Time 2	Time 3
MONOLINGUALS				
Year 1	Cito	Voc	Voc	Voc
Mo/NonMedia versus Mo/Media	Reading	Writing	*Writing	*Writing
	*Self Assessment			
	*Motivation/Attitude			
Year 3	Cito	*Voc	*Voc	*Voc
Mo/NonMedia versus Mo/Media	*Self Assessment	*Writing	*Writing	*Writing
	Motivation/Attitude			
BILINGUALS				
Year 1	Cito	Voc	Voc	*Voc
Bi/NonMedia versus Bi/Media	Reading	*Writing	Writing	Writing
	*Self Assessment			
	Motivation/Attitude			
Year 3	Cito	Voc	Voc	*Voc
Bi/NonMedia versus Bi/Media	*Self Assessment	Writing	*Writing	*Writing
	*Motivation/Attitude			

An asterisk indicates that for this measure there was a significant difference between the two groups that are being compared; Voc = vocabulary tests learners. Even though the first year Mo/NonMedia students assessed themselves lower in English proficiency than their Mo/Media counterparts, none of their lexical scores were significantly lower. Differences did start to occur in writing in the second test. In the third year, the Mo/NonMedia group scored significantly lower on self-assessment and on all lexical and writing tests compared to the Mo/Media group.

At first, the Bi/NonMedia and Bi/Media groups differed in their writing skills, but because this difference disappeared during the second and third test, we feel this initial difference may have been due to the fact that we were not able to test all the students immediately upon entering high school (some were about a month or two months in school at the time of the first tests). If we ignore the first writing test, we see that the pupils in the Bi/NonMedia group did assess themselves lower than their Bi/Media counterparts. In the third year, the students in the Bi/Non-Media group assessed themselves lower than their Bi/Media peers and also had less motivation, but it is not until the end of the third year that they started to lag behind their Bi/Media counterparts in the vocabulary and writing tests.

We may conclude that lack of media input had an effect on the proficiency levels of the non-media students, but the effects showed up at different times depending on what was being measured, that is, vocabulary knowledge or writing skills. For the first year students, the differences first showed up in the productive skills (writing). The third year students, however, scored lower on both receptive and productive skills.

One of the aims of this study was to find out to what extent the bilingual programme at the Reformed (non-media) school can compensate for the lack of input outside school. In Table 12 we compare the Bi/NonMedia group and the Mo/Media groups. The Bi/NonMedia group generally scored higher than

Table 12. Summary of differences between the bilingual non-media and monolingual media groups

	Measures at starting point	Time 1	Time 2	Time 3
Year 1 Bi/NonMedia versus Mo/Media	*Cito Reading Self Assessment Motivation/Attitude	Voc Writing	Voc Writing	Voc *Writing
Year 3 Bi/NonMedia versus Mo/Media	*Cito Self Assessment Motivation/Attitude	*Voc Writing	Voc Writing	Voc Writing

An asterisk indicates that for this measure there was a significant difference between the two groups that are being compared; Voc = vocabulary test the Mo/Media group. Asterisks denote significant differences in favor of the Bi/NonMedia group.

We may conclude that the Bi/NonMedia group was certainly able to keep up with the Mo/Media group. The Bi/NonMedia group even scored better on writing in the first year and on the lexical test in the third year. For the Reformed school, the bilingual programme has apparently been able to compensate for the lack of media input to a large extent, at least, compared to monolingual peers with media input. It would be interesting to see if they keep this advantage over time. According to the school though, the non-media bilingual groups now outscore their monolingual counterparts on English as a subject in the central examination that takes place in the Netherlands at the end of secondary school.

A final observation is that our data provide support for the idea that language input is not a static variable in the sense that it remains stable over time, but that it interacts with proficiency: with higher proficiency, out-of-school input may become more effective. Ideally, changes in input should be measured continuously in research such as reported on here, but measuring input is notoriously difficult in itself and continuous assessment makes this even more complex.

What this study has shown is that out of school contact with English is crucial for the development of proficiency. In English teaching more use could be made of that type of contact: relevant input from movies or video clips could be used for exercises in the classroom. Now it seems that the classroom and the world outside are kept strictly separate.

References

Berns, M., de Bot, K. & Hasebrink, U. (eds). 2007. *In the Presence of English. Media and European Youth.* Berlin: Springer.

Blondin, C., Candelier, M., Edelenbos, P., Johnstone, R., Kubanek-German, A. & Taeschner, T. 1998. *Foreign Languages in Primary and Pre-school Rducation. A Review of Recent Research within the European Union.* London: CILT.

Bonnet, G. 2004. *The Assessment of Pupils' Skills in English in Eight European Countries 2002.* Paris: European Network of policy makers for the evaluation of education systems.

Council of Europe. 2001. *Common European Framework of Reference for Languages: Learning, Teaching, Assessment.* Cambridge: CUP.

Edelenbos, P., Van der Schoot, F. & Verstralen, H. 2000. *Balans van het Engels aan het einde van de basisschool 2. Uitkomsten van de tweede peiling in 1996.* Arnhem: CITO-groep.

de Bot, K., Jagt, J., Janssen, H., Kessels, E. & Schils, E. 1986. Foreign television and language maintenance. *Second Language Research* 2: 72–82.

Elsen, A. 2009. Testing for Autonomy. PhD dissertation, University of Nijmegen.

Europees Platform. 2008. *Overzicht scholen primair onderwijs en voortgezet ondewijs met vroeg vreemde-talenonderwijs, versterkt talenonderwijs en tweetalig onderwijs in Nederland.* Haarlem: Europees Platform.

Gerritsen, M., Korzilius, H., van Meurs, F. & Gijsbers, I. 2000. English in Dutch commercials: Not understood and not appreciated. *Journal of Advertising Research* 40: 17–34.

Goorhuis-Brouwer, S. & de Bot, K. 2010. Early English language teaching in the Netherlands: The impact on first and second language acquisition. *International Journal of Bilingualism* 13.

Huibregtse, I. 2001. Effecten en Didactiek van Tweetalig Voortgezet Onderwijs in Nederland. PhD dissertation, University of Utrecht.

Huibregtse, I., Admiraal, W. & Meara, P. 2002. Scores on a yes-no vocabulary test: Correction for guessing and response style. *Language Testing* 19: 227–245.

Kuppens, A. 2007. De invloed van mediagebruik op de verwerving van Engelse woordenschat. Een empirische studie bij Vlaamse jongeren. *Tijdschrift voor Communicatiewetenschap* 35: 325–336.

Meara, P. & Buxton, B. 1987. An alternative to multiple choice vocabulary tests. *Language Testing* 4: 142–154.

NOS. 1977. *Ondertitelen of nasynchroniseren.* Hilversum: NOS B77-090.

Wilhelm, F. 1997. Foreign-Language teaching policy in the Netherlands 1800–1970: A historical outline. In *Perspectives on Foreign-language Policy: Studies in Honour of Theo van Els*, T. Bongaerts & K. de Bot (eds), 1–20. Amsterdam: John Benjamins.

Index

In the *AILA Applied Linguistics Series* the following titles have been published thus far or are scheduled for publication:

8 **DE HOUWER, Annick and Antje WILTON (eds.):** English in Europe Today. Sociocultural and educational perspectives. 2011. xi, 170 pp.

7 **DALTON-PUFFER, Christiane, Tarja NIKULA and Ute SMIT (eds.):** Language Use and Language Learning in CLIL Classrooms. 2010. x, 295 pp.

6 **ARONIN, Larissa and Britta HUFEISEN (eds.):** The Exploration of Multilingualism. Development of research on L3, multilingualism and multiple language acquisition. 2009. vii, 167 pp.

5 **GIBBONS, John and M. Teresa TURELL (eds.):** Dimensions of Forensic Linguistics. 2008. vi, 316 pp.

4 **FORTANET-GÓMEZ, Inmaculada and Christine A. RÄISÄNEN (eds.):** ESP in European Higher Education. Integrating language and content. 2008. vi, 285 pp.

3 **MAGNAN, Sally Sieloff (ed.):** Mediating Discourse Online. 2008. vii, 364 pp.

2 **PRINSLOO, Mastin and Mike BAYNHAM (eds.):** Literacies, Global and Local. 2008. vii, 218 pp.

1 **LAMB, Terry and Hayo REINDERS (eds.):** Learner and Teacher Autonomy. Concepts, realities, and response. 2008. vii, 286 pp.